CREATIVE DESIGNS IN FURNITURE

Featuring 125 of

America's Leading

Craft Artists

Kraus Sikes Inc.

CREATIVE DESIGNS IN FURNITURE

Creative Designs in Furniture
is a publication of:

Kraus Sikes Inc.
228 State Street
Madison, WI 53703
608-256-1990
800-969-1556

ISBN 0-9616012-9-9
Distribution: This book is exclusively distributed by
Rockport Publishers Inc., Rockport, Massachusetts

Writers: Bill Kraus, Susan Troller, Jay Rath
Editors: Toni Sikes, Karen Stocker
Design: Karen Szczepkowski, Kristine Firchow
Production: Design Communications
Color separation, printing and binding: Toppan Printing Co.
Printed in Singapore

Front Cover Photo: Gary Upton, audio system; photo by James Marks
Title Page Photo: Joel W. Evett & Robert L. Boylen, Pompeii Cabinet; photo by A. Dean Powell

Divider Page Photos:
Furniture in Wood — Lynette Breton and Ann Flannery, white oak desk; photo by John Tanabe

Furniture in Mixed Media — Neophile, El Noche table and Chevron mirror

Painted Furniture — Alphonse Mattia, burning table lamps

Architectural Woodwork — Tony Clarke, wet bar; photo by Scott Miles

CONTENTS

Introduction

Why custom-designed, handcrafted furniture?

Why custom-designed, handcrafted furniture, you may ask, when furniture showrooms and home furnishing stores are already meeting consumer demands for variety? There are quite a few reasons, some quite practical and others esoteric.

Artist-designed furniture brings you more choices...

A look through these pages will open up a whole world of furniture that cannot be found in the furniture showrooms and home furniture stores. The 125 artists featured in this book reflect the enormous diversity of today's craft field. Here you will see furniture that is made of traditional materials using traditional techniques alongside pieces made in unexpected ways with innovative materials. Anything and everything is possible.

Artist-designed furniture gives you better value...

We don't tell you that one-of-a-kind furniture is less expensive, although it is not necessarily more expensive, than manufactured furniture. We will tell you that this furniture is a bargain in quality. Craft artists take old-world pride in what they create, and the result is workmanship that takes your breath away.

Artists can design something just for you...

The ultimate luxury is having something made just for you. When you commission an artist to design and make a piece of furniture, you become a part of the design process. You can select an artist with a style that reflects your individual taste, and you can work with this artist to produce furniture that is right for your specific environment. The artist will pay particular attention to the physical and aesthetic needs of your space, and the financial needs of your budget.

Working with artists directly will put you in touch with people who have spent their lives making beautiful things. They truly care about quality of work and service to customers.

This book pays tribute to a significant design revolution — the American Studio Movement — and to the craft artists whose work is supporting that movement.

Toni Fountain Sikes

Explosion of Choices

An explosion of choices faces today's furniture buyer. To a large extent, the array of possibilities exists because of the creative designs of studio furniture makers. These craft artists offer a profusion of styles, exquisite materials, one-of-a-kind pieces, tailor-made to fit the individual personalities of the contemporary home, corporate setting, or public space.

This book highlights the great variety and talents of the leading American craft artists who are creating beautiful furniture for today and the heirlooms of tomorrow. As you journey through these pages, allow your imagination to enter the realm of furniture built specifically for you and your particular needs.

Everything from a reproduction of a favorite Chippendale chair to a decorative sculptural piece is possible. Hand–crafted furniture can be designed to meet both your functional and aesthetic needs, while providing a unique gift to pass on to future generations.

Furniture designers build on the work created by artisans centuries ago. In Egypt, 6,000 years past, furniture was inlaid with gold and ivory, and animal forms were incorporated into the design. In the Renaissance and afterward, furniture became increasingly ornamented as designers sought to create more and more "artistic" work. At the beginning of this century, American designers emphasized a return to simplicity.

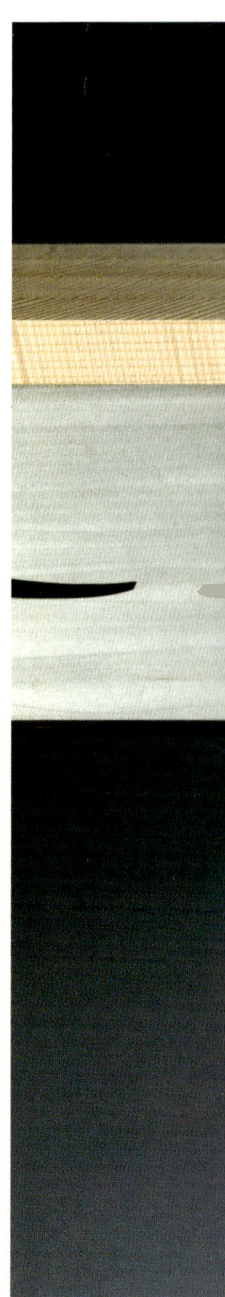

Today, all forms are grist for the mill. As we move into the next century, furniture will increasingly reflect the designers' values, and perhaps even societal concerns. Hand–crafted furniture reflects our tastes, and allows us to say something about who we are, or who we want to be.

Originality of design and the care that can only be imparted by the craftsman's hand are qualities we have learned to cherish. The only limitation for the furniture artist is the shape of the human body and the inquisitiveness of the human mind.

Jamie Robertson
Running dog table, curly hardwood veneer, poplar dyed blue, ebony inlay, laquer finish, 36"Hx52"Wx18"D.
▼

SEARCHING FOR THE ESSENCE OF WOOD:
Michael Emmons

Michael Emmons of Big Sur, California, believes, "With any artistic venture, the depth of your involvement in it determines the aesthetic qualities. Your relationship with the materials, especially with furniture, is important. The pieces take on form by themselves."

"I started out in the late 60s as a jeweler," Emmons relates. "But I wanted to work on bigger pieces, and I also had a home that needed furniture. I started with a traditional Adirondack chair, and after a few tries, I came up with a design that was comfortable. Friends started asking me to make chairs for them, and I found that I really enjoyed working with live green wood. I came up with several designs for willow furniture, and I feel I took it as far as I could."

Emmons says, "Eucalyptus is very abundant and is a significant wood for Big Sur. I started developing designs with Eucalyptus to bring out the essence of the nature of the wood into expression."

He feels this technique is helped by using antique tools. "There is a spirit in old tools which completes the process. I'm using one tool that's over a hundred years old. It's so well made, it seems like new. Yet it has a spirit that complements the design of the furniture."

"Sometimes," Emmons continues, "I feel that I'm a tool for the wood's expression."

Who Are These Artists?

Just who are these artists? They come from widely diverse backgrounds and training. Many have finely-honed skills in the traditional craft fields of woodworking and metalsmithing. Others have moved into furniture making from associated areas, such as sculpture, painting, architecture and industrial design.

The individuals covered in this book are by no means a comprehensive listing of artists working in furniture, but as a group they represent the diversity of the American furniture movement. Within their varied disciplines are contrasts and similarities dictated not so much by the furniture itself but by materials and creative design approaches.

*Larry White
Armoire, curly maple, wenge, satiner, 42"Hx60"Wx20"D.*
▼

◄ Grady Mathews
Blanket chest, eastern hard
maple, birdseye maple, ebony
and aromatic cedar,
18"Hx36"Wx18"D.

▲ Colin Reid
Sideboard, wenge/curly maple,
88"Lx30"Hx20"D.

11

THE FURNITURE MAKER'S RESPONSIBILITY TO THE ENVIRONMENT:
Gary Upton

Environmental concerns influence much of Gary Upton's furniture making. He's been exploring for years the use of mixing materials, such as brass, aluminum and stones with hardwoods, because of a personal concern he shares with other artists about the use and abuse of the rainforests in tropical countries. Upton responds, "It's a shame that so much is destroyed...but furniture makers are conscious to these concerns. That's why WARP — Woodworkers Alliance for the Protection of Rain Forests was formed. I feel that as a woodworker, it's my responsibility to be aware of how my work effects the environment and to support sustainable developments and reforested areas. I'm relying more on domestic woods, but when clients do request exotics, I charge an additional fee for this which is donated to nonprofit projects, such as WARP."

In addition, mixing materials, such as granite and aluminum, requires different techniques which effects the creative process of furniture design. "It's exciting...real tricky and difficult...you have to find that sensitive balance. It's a challenge," says Upton. He finds that these materials can improve the function of the piece and they work well for contemporary, architectural designs which is the direction his work is taking.

But perhaps, most important to Gary Upton, is the responsibility he faces as a furniture maker, "The beauty of the furniture creates a positive experience, but I also need to combine this awareness with a conscious education of the materials."

New Design Freedom

What unites this rather eclectic group is a new design freedom. Methods and materials certainly matter. Functionality is important. But a wonderful wealth of imagination has been unleashed, and the American public is the beneficiary.

Simplicity is still important, and new materials and designs have shattered traditional expectations. Colors can be outrageously bright; form can be exaggerated. Meanwhile, wicker and rattan, as well as other traditional materials, have not been lost. But familiar wood tones are being used as painters might use their pigments. These craft artists select materials and forms to excite the senses and compel an emotional response.

More than ever before, artists are bringing their talents and views of the world to furniture. Only two decades ago, this movement was individual. Artists defined their own needs and found their own inspirations. Now there is a fuller dialogue, brought about by the awakening to the possibilities in furniture.

There has been a virtual explosion in the numbers and styles of furniture makers which has resulted in a mind-boggling expansion of what is available in this last decade of the 20th century. It is an exciting time in the development of the American furniture movement.

Once we accept the challenge of the artist's vision, who knows where these designers may lead us?

Furniture makers are helping us rediscover the personal significance of the items that fill our homes and work places. No longer satisfied with clones and uniformity, we are looking for much more.

This range of choices in contemporary furniture design provides a new freedom. Originally made by hand by artisans, furniture was largely abandoned to the assembly line during the Industrial Age. Today, the large, new generation of artists creating furniture frees us from assembly-line conformity. They have succeeded in broadening our concept of furniture – at a time when society is searching for basic means of individual expression.

▶

Alphonse Mattia
"Primates" valet, 1986, bleached
and stained ash and poplar,
74"Hx18"Wx18"D.

◀ *Mark Nichols*
"Crushed Groove", 1988, hot
forged steel, brass trim on Spanish
granite, 20"Hx24"Wx24"D.

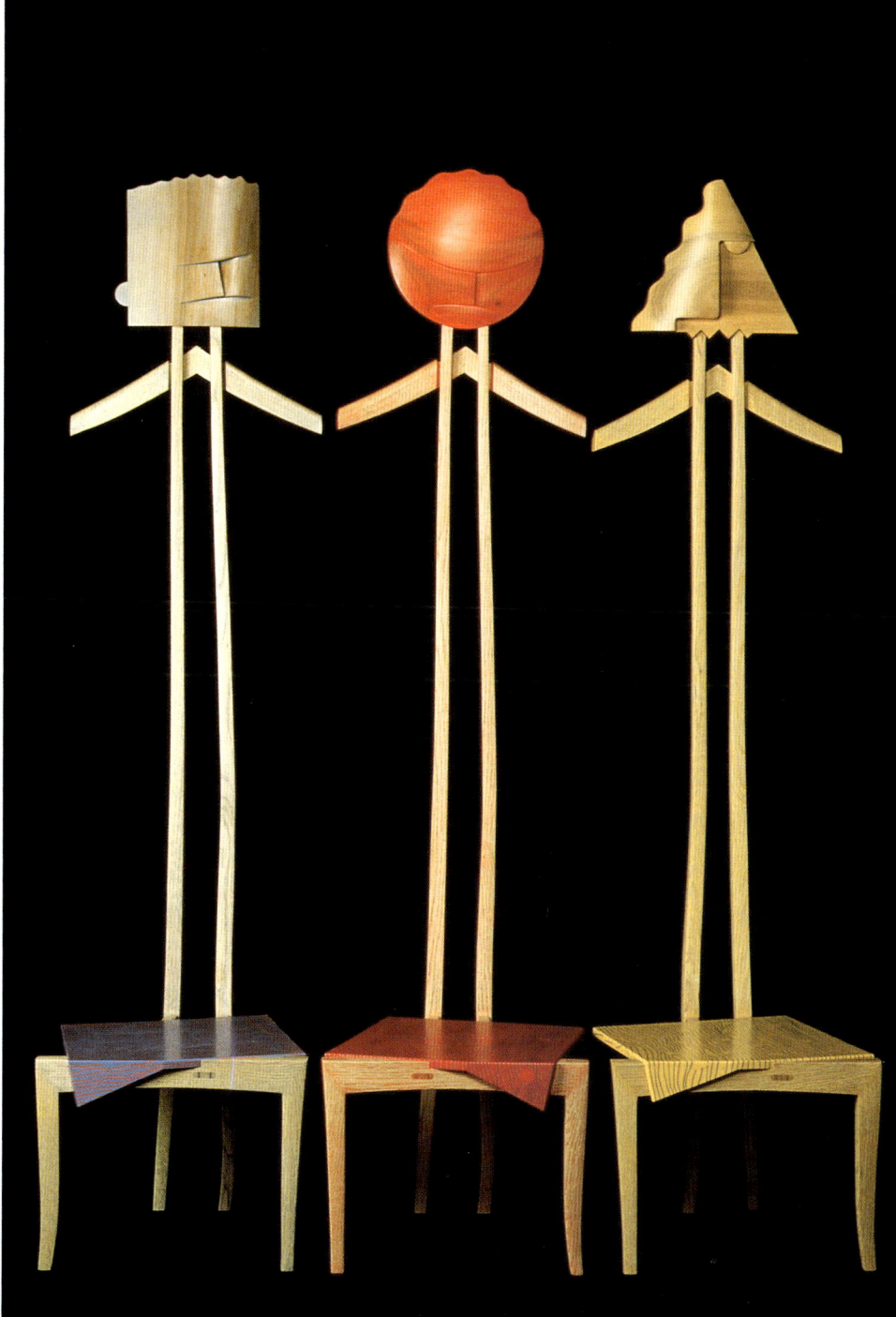

Exploring the Border Between Craft and Art:
Johanna Okovic Goodman

Johanna Okovic Goodman finds beauty in existing wood chairs. She creates whimsical pieces by adding ribbon, fabric, beads, hemp, oil cloth and handmade paper to these chairs to mimic the bodies of animals.

For the Philadelphia artist, the use of existing chairs highlights qualities in all chairs, and our relationships to them.

"I think of it as an armature for a person, like a frame on a painting," she states. This framework is not a limitation, but simply one of the medium's conventions. By making reference to those conventions, she hopes to explore the hazy border between craft and art.

"I like the idea of chairs, because they're always taken for granted," she says. "There's the connection to something that's ordinary and trying to make it extraordinary that is appealing to me."

Even on the most basic level, Okovic Goodman's chairs are intended to incite a response. She strives to put color into homes and to get others to see objects in a new way — to think about them.

"It's also a way of having people who may not understand art touch it. They may not go to an art museum. They may not know about art. But it's something they can relate to. More people want to be close to art, rather than have it be stuck away somewhere. It helps bridge a gap, in a way."

"A chair for me has always been significant," says Okovic Goodman. "Ever since I was a child. Everyone has their chair. So it's something that has a personal quality and comfortableness."

The Lowly Chair

◀
Dennis Proksa
Wrought iron chair with leaf back.

Take the lowly chair. We project our moods and personalities by the chairs we sit in. In one mood a big, fat chair is just right; in another mood, a rocking chair. Our purposes for sitting are often very different. People sit back and muse; people sit formally waiting for dinner to be served.

A setting that is full of chairs, all slightly different, immediately creates an atmosphere of rich experience, moods and personalities. Artists are helping us here by introducing fresh ideas, inventive techniques, and an artist's eye and view to the world. What they can do with four legs, a seat and a back boggles the mind!

▶
Daniel Mack
Sugar maple side chair with upholstered seat, 1989, 45"Hx17"Dx25"W.

◄   *Colin Reid*
Yellow satinwood dining chair,
22"x32"x18".

▶
Robert Erickson
Martinez recliner, Oregon ash,
ebony and black leather,
33"Wx42"Hx42"L.

FURNITURE THAT MAKES A STATEMENT:
Eric Bergman

Eric Bergman, a New York City artist/designer, is more inclined toward furniture with explicit statements.

"First of all I was a visual artist," Bergman says. "Then I studied industrial design, with the thinking that approaching the masses was more of a thing to do these days in our society. Some of the traditional art forms weren't making that jump."

Furniture that truly interacts with its users is an opportunity Bergman saw. "I think I have a greater chance getting to more people by designing a table versus doing a painting," Bergman states. "I think that has a lot to do with why I'm doing furniture. I'm still experimenting with how far I can go with it, in terms of making artistic statements with objects — functional objects — and how far people are willing to look at objects as things that make a statement. I think if you're going to call something a table, it has to function as a table," he says. "But I want it to have this additional information on it."

Broadening the Concept

So, what is furniture? Artists know that furniture is much more than arms, legs, platforms, backs, shelves and drawers. Certainly, the furniture we live with must satisfy the most basic needs of supporting activities, such as sleeping, eating, resting, writing, thinking. But we are coming to understand that the furniture we surround ourselves with is much more than merely functional.

Some people may choose a single hand-crafted piece and make it the focal point of a living room. Here it is free to draw attention and make a statement. In the boardroom, several pieces can be combined to work in harmony to create a unified statement of credibility, trust and a high level of craftsmanship.

A common thread that weaves its way through this philosophy of furniture design is the interaction with people's minds, as well as their bodies. John Ruskin wrote, "Fine art is that in which the hand, the head and heart of man go together." This is the theme that can be found today, and it is what raises furniture design from the level of craft to that of an art form.

.... of Furniture

Like all artists and craftsmen, furniture designers also seek an audience for their work. To reflect society, the pieces must be part of it. The interaction, at times, can be organic to the work's creation. Commissioned furniture provides the opportunity to work with a designer through the process of creation, to bask proudly in the reflected glow of the furniture's high degree of craftsmanship, its one-of-a-kind design and sensuality. In this respect, the cost — though roughly comparable to high quality factory goods and generally less than an expensive antique — is of lesser significance than the satisfaction of being involved in the process of creative design.

Craig Nutt
Pepper table, 1989, birch inlay with dyed wood, carved and laquered wood, 30"Wx17"Dx26"H.
▼

▲ *Michael Hurwitz*
Chaise lounge on rockers, 7$\frac{1}{2}$'x3'x2'.

◀ *Jamie Robertson*
Shelves, pau amarillo, carved ebony, oil finish, 78"Hx46"Wx11"D.

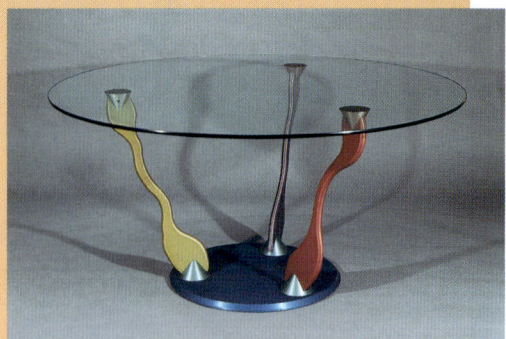

FURNITURE AS A METAPHOR:
Peter Handler

Peter Handler, a furniture designer who works in Philadelphia, feels he is an artist who speaks to his times.

"I want somebody 30 years from now to look at my work from this period and say, 'Boy, that's real '90s work,'" Handler says. "I don't really believe in art or in design that anything is timeless, or should be. I think that any piece of art is a product of its times. Periods of art and design are metaphorical images of a period. My work reflects this thinking. That is one of my goals: that my furniture looks like it's coming out at the end of the twentieth century."

"I guess it's similar, in a way, to the way a car is designed," says Peter Handler. "You have the chassis, or armature, and the function is built in. And then what is designed within those parameters is the beauty of the pieces. You can call that a limit, if you like to, in that it's a starting point. It's sort of like being given an assignment, only it's giving it to oneself.

"With sculpture, it only needs to be something you look at and it won't fall over. In furniture, the elements have to work, have permanence, and look good. You create, in a visual sense, a flow that creates harmony. My desire in a piece of furniture — what I want to accomplish when I make a single piece — is to design something that people will enjoy. My object is to create work that makes a difference in a small way, that contributes to somebody's happiness. The feeling of harmony is important in that consideration."

"The stimulus for my work has been technology," Handler says. "In a very broad sense, I've felt for some time technology is probably the strongest force in changing the nature of our society. And what I've wanted to do with my work is create images that give a feeling of humanized technology. That is, I don't want my work to look like the Starship Enterprise. I want it to suggest that move into technology without looking like it. So it suggests it. It's a metaphor."

The Dialogue Continues...

The point is that we have never had this many alternatives. It is astonishing that the simple chair, table and bed can have so many variations and still meet the single, great, over-arching criterion: the comfort of the human body.

Perhaps the only unifying force within the furniture movement today is the opportunity for individual expression and the search for the functional and artistic meaning in each piece. As this dialogue continues, we will find that furniture can continue to comfort us while enhancing our spaces to create our own unique home and work environments.

▲ *Rosanne Somerson*
Tall back chairs, 1990, curly maple, pau ferro silk and patenated bronze, 60"Hx21"Wx 20"D, Peter Joseph collection.

Beeken/Parsons ▶
Music stand, white oak with adjustable music rest, 60"Hx26"W.

Rosanne Somerson
"Leg-o-saurus" bench, 1990,
cherry, macassar ebony
and tapestry fabric,
18^1/$_4$"Hx55"Wx17^1/$_2$"D. ▶

Craig Nutt ▶
Braswell bed, full-size, 1989,
cherry, 90"Lx59"Wx44"H.

The New American Furniture Store

We all know how to find the local furniture store and how to shop there. This book is an introduction to a new kind of furniture store – one that is stocked by the work of a large and growing collection of craft artists instead of by manufacturers. This furniture store exists in the mind not in a particular place, and you cannot shop it in the traditional way.

Here you will find the work of over 100 furniture makers who will be happy to sell you what they have made or to make something specifically for you and your space and your taste. These artists represent the vanguard of the "American Studio Movement." They are, of course, artists, but they are also professional, competent business people who, whether they work alone or with others, deliver on time and as specified and back up their work with all the traditional guarantees that other sources of furniture are likely to provide.

They are, however, a little harder to find. They are not likely to be on Main Street, and they are never in the mall. This furniture store in the mind is spread all over the country. Its occupants are found in books such as this one, in magazines like Fine Woodworking, at craft fairs both large and small, in craft galleries in the larger cities, by word of mouth, and, yes, in some yellow pages which have a section titled "Furniture Designers And Custom Builders" or something akin.

The reasons for shopping this fragmented and scattered store are many and varied. When you shop this store you are looking not just for the right furniture, but for the only chair, the only cabinet, the only bed, the only table that will work for your unique needs and style. While the studio movement includes the work of artists who do what is called "production" work, even their production work is unique, because it is not produced by headless hands. Every piece is handmade; every piece is different, even if it is ever so slightly different.

FUNCTIONAL FURNITURE WITHOUT AN ARTISTIC MESSAGE:
Ronald Puckett

Ronald Puckett, a Virginia furniture designer, "paints" his pieces by using the colors and textures of wood. He begins with sketching shapes and forms, drawing on significant historical design concepts, his clients' preferences, and architecture around his hometown of Richmond.

"Most of the time, people come to me because they've seen something I've done. They already like the basic design or elements of my work," says Puckett. "If they want to combine elements, I'll go back and design something else."

"As far as the wood, usually I look for some sort of contrast. To me," Puckett relates, "the contrast of those colors is another added detail of the piece. In selecting the wood, there are a couple of different things to consider. I always look for colors that work together. Also, grain makes a difference. Otherwise, it really boils down to color. I end up using dark woods as accent quite a bit."

Beyond that, Puckett's designs reflect his conscious and unconscious artistic tastes. He offers no messages, and does not feel comfortable making furniture for art's sake. "I like making furniture for furniture's sake. But at the same time it can be a piece of art as well. Function is the most important consideration," says Puckett. His patrons desire practicality as well as beauty, and happily, the artist's tastes coincide with his clients'.

While everything displayed in this book is for sale, most of the things in this book have probably already been sold. If a shopper is using this book with an eye to buying something, the shopper is probably not going to get the piece pictured. The shopper of this new furniture store must understand that a close but not exact replica can be made. Or, better yet, a collaboration with the artist whose style the shopper is drawn to can be commissioned to create something unique.

Here is the main difference between the stores we are accustomed to shopping in and this new furniture store. This store is more diverse, more individual, and most of the work in it is commissionable. The traditional store has a large selection of colors and materials and even styles. In this store the styles are unique to the artists on view, and once a style is selected, everything and anything becomes possible, because, while you can buy what has been made or a similar clone of what has been made, you can also commission a piece of furniture that is unique.

Commissioning sounds like something mayors and monument committees do. Commissioning furniture is a lot less self-important, bureaucratic, and costly; and it is a lot more fun.

◀ *Daniel Mack*
Left: Forest arm chair, maple with Shaker woven seat, 1989, 45"Hx20"Dx25"W.
Right: Dancing wishbone chair, maple with Shaker woven seat, 1989, 56"H.

Shopping This New Store

There is more to shopping this new store than driving out to the mall on the beltline. You have to find these people. The first thing to do is to scan the field, before you proceed to the next most obvious step of selecting the right artist. The selection is the decision from which all others will flow, so it's worth devoting time and study to this choice and to season the process with both wild artistic hopes and hard-nosed realism.

Whoever is making the decision, there are several ways to find the right artist, most of which have been enumerated earlier. Make your initial selection on the basis of what you like about an artist's work that you have seen in person or in print. When you make the first contact, either via telephone or a letter, be prepared to provide information about the piece of furniture you are looking for, the budget, and even the materials and colors you have in mind (if, indeed, you do have those in mind). If you do, this will help the artist tailor his or her response more specifically to you, which will yield a better sense of whether this is the right person for your project.

▲ *Breton Flannery Woodworks*
White oak desk with aqua latilla
inlay, 30"Hx20"Dx60"L.

▲ *Beth Forer*
Ceramic tile on wood, table
detail —Mishima technique.

Most experienced craft artists will be pleased to provide you with a portfolio – usually on slides, but sometimes in a brochure. Don't, however, expect to see the exact piece you're looking for in a portfolio. Remember, you're choosing an artist at this point, not a piece of furniture. Look for creativity, command of the materials or technology, and also how the work seems to fit your specific environment.

Choosing an artist is much like choosing a real estate agent or some other professional, for that matter, an architect or designer. If it feels like you might have trouble working together, it's wise to heed these early warning signs. But if all goes well and you decide to move ahead with the artist, you should move ahead in agreeing on a budget and timetable and signing a contract or a letter of agreement.

It is a good idea to put the commission in writing. The artist will present you with a proposal, including a payment schedule, that you can discuss, agree to, and sign before the work commences. The idea is to, in effect, get the legalities out of the way early to avoid problems later on. It seems a little formal in what is a personal collaboration, but suffer it; it's worth it. A letter of agreement will assure you that the artist will complete his or her work on time and to specifications. It will also assure the artist that he or she will get paid the right amount at the right time.

Payment to the artist customarily is made in three stages. The first payment usually is made when the contract is signed. It covers the artist's time and creativity in developing a design specific to your needs. You can expect to go through several rounds of trial and error in the design process, but at the end you will come up with something that everyone agrees upon.

If the commission is cancelled during the design period, the artist keeps the money already paid for work performed.

The second payment is generally set for a mid-way point in the project and is for work done to date. If the materials are expensive, the client may be asked to advance money at this stage to cover materials costs. Final payment usually is due when the work is delivered.

FINDING A NICHE — CUSTOM FINE WOOD PIECES:
Ron Diefenbacher

Ron Diefenbacher, a St. Louis furniture maker, works by himself. Though there are lots of temptations to go into production work, or built-ins, he decided that he needed to specialize. His niche — custom, free-standing, fine wood furniture.

Diefenbacher says, "People come to me with a specific need whether that be an individual client, an interior designer or an architect. Most of my work is through commissions — like the card table I'm working on right now for an architect."

My artistic philosophy is evolving. Ten years ago I was strongly influenced by Shaker, Chinese and Scandinavian styles. Now it is more subconscious. I frequently start with a single element — like a leg of a table, a curved piece — from that spark I build a design as you would build a house. I'd say my style is contemporary, rather than reproductions or preservations."

Diefenbacher continues, "Today I focus on the use of North American woods, such as English walnut, cherry and ash. And use exotic woods for detail and secondary pieces. Since this exotic wood comes from sensitive rain forests, there is a concern which I share with other artists that we may be contributing to the abuse of this area. It's not a closed issue. We're still waiting for a fuller understanding to determine what is the real problem in the rain forests."

In addition to these personal and global developments, Diefenbacher says, "The furniture movement today can be described as eclectic. People are going in a variety of directions. Artistic expression is acceptable in many different ways. I think this is good for the consumer. There is a lot of original work coming out now. You couldn't say these things ten or fifteen years ago. It's an exciting time in furniture design and the future promises to offer more variety and choices."

◄ *Kevin Early
"Water Table" writing desk —
Spanish cedar, maple and dyed
veneer inlay.*

A commission takes full advantage
of the possibilities of this new kind of
way to buy furniture. The other
options that take advantage of the
new store — shopping craft fairs,
scouring the craft galleries, plumbing
the literature that features this kind of
work — are more widely used and
almost as satisfying. No matter how
you prefer to shop, try the new store.
You'll love it.

◄ *Alphonse Mattia*
Scary bench, 1989, purple heart,
red oak, suede, aluminum leaf,
90"x24"x18".

FURNITURE IN WOOD

Lincoln Alden

Alden Design
Route 132
S. Strafford, VT 05070
(800) 562-5110
(802) 765-4314

Designer and furnituremaker Lincoln Alden specializes in creating distinctive tables uniting stone and wood. Fine hardwoods are selected for color and grain to accent the natural beauty of polished marble and granite insets. With over 40 stone choices from around the world, clients can specify color and texture to suit any residential or corporate setting. Integrity in construction and simplicity in line reveal the quiet elegance of Alden Design furniture.

Prices start at $900.00 for cocktail tables. Delivery time ranges from 2–4 months. Design consultation, brochure and stone samples available upon request.

(Left) Cocktail table, 24"w x 40"l x 17"h, walnut, curly rose marble.

(Right) Writing desk, 35"w x 50"l x 30"h, cherry, walnut inlay, Vermont Verde Antique marble.

James A. Bacigalupi
Bacigalupi Studios
#4 140 Lewis Road
San Jose, CA 95111
(408) 225-8303
(408) 225-9102 FAX

Bacigalupi Studios design and manufacture limited production and one-of-a-kind furniture and accessories for residential, commercial, and religious purposes.

All manner of materials are used including glass, metal, wood, stone and concrete.

Prices available upon request.

Peter Barrett

Peter Barrett-Furniture Design
RR#1, Box 1434
Pownal, ME 04069
(207) 688-4915

Peter Barrett designs and builds one-of-a-kind and limited production furniture for the home and office. His furniture is of simple line, built to the highest standards and displays a timeless elegance. Woods are selected for color, texture and graining, often combining contrasting woods to accentuate the lines of a piece and to punctuate details. Commissions and collaborations are welcome.

Portfolio and pricelist available upon request.

(Left) Display cabinet, pearwood, rosewood, holly, 20½ x 15½ x 73.

(Top right) Console table, quilted maple, rosewood, pearwood, 38½ x 17 x 30. Mirror, pearwood, rosewood, 38 x 18.

(Bottom right) Console table detail.

Christian H. Becksvoort

P.O. Box 12
New Gloucester, ME 04260
(207) 926-4608

Christian Becksvoort specializes in tables, chairs, cabinets and desks which are individually built to the highest standards. The unity of form and timeless simplicity make this furniture you can live with, appropriate for today as well as years to come.

Commissions and small productions. Prices from $300 to $10,000. Delivery time 3 to 6 months.

Brochure $5.00.

Bruce Beeken
Jeff Parsons

Beeken/Parsons
Shelburne Farms
Shelburne, VT 05482
(802) 985-2913

"Bruce Beeken and Jeff Parsons comprise a partnership that brings together the technical sophistication and efficiency of a production shop and the expressive qualities of one-off studio work. Seeking the flexibility to undertake production jobs, exhibition work or, ideally, a combination of both, they have achieved a rare balance of productivity, personal involvement and experimentation that integrates technical and esthetic concerns in an economically viable fashion. Their constant interplay between stripped-down form and production methods such as shaping and bending enable them to develop subtle designs the simplicity of which belies considerable conceptual depth."— Edward S. Cooke/Assistant Curator of American Decorative Arts and Sculpture/Museum of Fine Arts Boston

Child's Bed/Sycamore, Maple, Chromed Brass; Silk Cording, Acrylic Sailcloth, Cotton and Silk Futon.

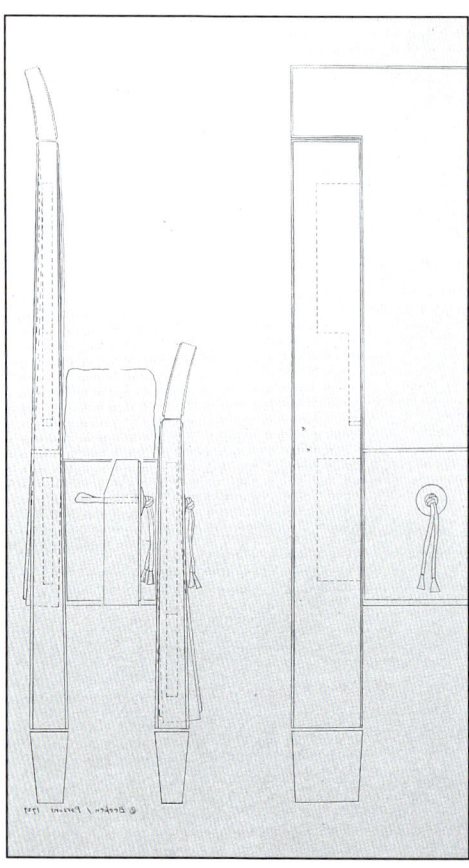

Carter Gustav Blocksma

Designforms
15675 Gorton Road
Grass Lake, MI 49240
(313) 475-8751
FAX; (313) 475-0350

Carter Blocksma has been designing and manufacturing furniture and cabinetry for over fifteen years. His company produces custom and limited production pieces for residential and commercial application nation-wide. Blocksma's work has been recognized by "Fine Woodworking" and exhibited at the "International Furniture Fair" in New York.

Prices range from $900.00 to several thousand depending on the complexity of the commission. Allow 8–12 weeks for delivery once a blueprint (or model) and price contract have been settled.

Architectural and interior design collaboration is encouraged.

Additional information available.

RECENT COMMISSIONS

Giorgio Armani, IL

TRW Building, MI

Hobbs & Black Architects, MI

Matthew C. Hoffmann Jewelers, NY

(Below, right) "Deco Drama" 49" x 24" x 80" Mahogany, Wenge, Sapele Veneer, Curly Maple.

(Bottom left) "Dancing Chairs" 21" x 21" x 36" White Oak, Curly Bubinga.

Mark T. Bolesky

Custom Carpentry
154 N. Diamond Street
Mansfield, OH 44902
(419) 526-9663

The creation of our limited production furniture is accomplished through the mind of the designer and the hands of our master craftsman.

Mediums include wood, glass, stone and man-made materials available in any finish specified. Bolesky excels in reproductions, residential and commercial works on a limited production basis.

Fine workmanship, quality materials, limited production by three master craftsmen in our studio. We work closely with you in creating that special furniture that will fit your vision and space.

Brochure and promotional video available for $12.

(Top) White oak and wenge inlayed cedar chests with dovetail joints.

(Bottom) One-of-a-kind exotic and native wood table. Signed and numbered in 18k gold.

Jim Braverman

Jim Alexander Braverman Fine Furniture
P.O. Box 2482
Aptos, CA 95001
(408) 662-9402

Jim Braverman's furniture is recognized for its simple elegance and high degree of adaptability. Incorporating the finest of technique and material, each piece produced is structurally sound and exquisitely detailed. Having furnished numerous homes in their entirety, his experience in design and collaboration is extensive. (References available.)

Working within a scheduled framework of commissions, limited production and collaborative design projects, Braverman produces furniture, as well as light fixtures for both home and office. Allow three to six months from point of contact to delivery.

Portfolio, price list and further information available upon request.

(Top right) Chest, 42"w x 23"h x 20"d, ash, wenge and ebony.

(Bottom right) Entry table, 55"w x 30"h x 17"d, ash and ebony.

(Left) Dining set: table, 76"w x 38"h x 31"h; chairs, 17"w x 46"h x 18"d. Both made of koa and ebony.

Cedar lined, sliding tray inside

Marble inlay

Lynette Breton
Ann Flannery

Breton Flannery Woodworks
10 South Street
Freeport, ME 04032
(207) 865-4142

Lynette Breton and Ann Flannery formed their business in 1985, after 20 years of combined experience. Each trained in the West separately coming East to nurture their love for the traditional forms of furniture and wooden boat building. After romancing that part of their careers, they formed Breton Flannery Woodworks. Their focus is the union between traditional construction methods with designs of today, to create antiques of tomorrow.

Specializing in custom woodwork and design, their work includes high quality built-ins, solid wood furniture, doors and staircasing.

The chair pictured here was recently honored by being selected from 10,000 photographs for the cover of Fine Woodworking Design Book Five.

Please write or call for more information.

Southwestern style twin headboard and table.

Southwestern style end chest, 32"w.x 26"h.x20"d.

Southwestern style reading chair, 19"w.x 41"h.x19 1/2"d.

40

Wayne Brungard

Wayne Brungard - Architectural Elements
4801 Oxford Road
Longmont, CO 80503
(303) 443-4801

Wayne Brungard places special emphasis on the creation of architectural elements of unique design that fulfill functional needs and provide lasting appeal. With the careful choice of materials—domestic or imported wood, fabricated or cast bronze, stainless steel, Cor-Ten, glass, granite or marble—Brungard can create an impressive selection of finished pieces, including desks, tables, entrance doors, entrance gates, cabinets, screens or sculptures.

His work has been referred to as functional sculpture. Recognized by architects and designers for the high quality of design and craftsmanship, his work has been shown and collected nationally.

Michael Cabaniss

P. O. Box 142
Davenport, CA 95017
(408) 426-4819 or (408) 426-9418

The artist, through the skillful knowledge of his tools and craft, has forged a body of work that speaks quietly about comfort and function and the natural beauty of wood.

To achieve structural integrity, dovetail and mortise-and-tenon joinery is utilized. All parts are interlocked together, then pinned or lightly glued. Great attention is also given to design that accommodates the seasonal expansion and contraction of wood.

Every piece is dated and identified by the artist's hand-carved signature.

All inquiries are invited.

(Right) *BUREAU #2*, 54 X 36 X 24 inches, Black Walnut, Peroba Rosa, Gabon Ebony, Aromatic Red Cedar.

Photography is by Tony Grant of Santa Cruz, California.

James M. Camp

J. Camp Designs
11 Longford Street
Philadelphia, PA 19136
(215) 333-9060
(215) 333-2899

J. Camp designs and executes functional sculptured wood pieces for home and business. The unique works are primarily done in walnut with hand-rubbed linseed oil finish to highlight the natural beauty of the wood. Other woods made available upon request. Camp specializes in cocktail and game tables. In addition music stands, stools, and other one-of-a-kind pieces may be commissioned. J. Camp is well known in the Philadelphia area with 25 years of experience in the field. The artist is available for consultation. There is a design fee. Prices range from $1,500–$10,000.

(Top) Spine Back Rocker

(Lower) Chess Age II

John Clark

823 Arlington Street
Jackson, MS 39202
(601) 948-4740

New departures from traditional forms and imaginative use of innovative materials characterize John Clark's furniture. He combines precise joinery with a variety of uncommon materials to produce distinctive pieces for homes and offices.

John earned his MFA in furniture design from the Program in Artisanry at Boston University. His work has appeared in several national publications and can be found in principal galleries and collections throughout the country.

Commissioned works vary appropriately in price, but most pieces are $1500–$4000 retail. Budget and delivery considerations are consistently honored. Detailed portfolio information and specific responses to inquiries are promptly provided.

Conference table, desk, bookcase, and moldings for a private office

End tables for an executive office reception area: bleached cherry, granite, purpleheart

(left) "Tall Table": bleached mahogany, purpleheart, Nevamar solid surface   (right) "Orbit Table": bleached mahogany, purpleheart, anodized aluminum, sandblasted glass

Tony Clarke

Clarke Fine Furniture
One Cottage Street 5th Floor
Easthampton, MA 01027
(413) 527-2127

Tony Clarke offers a wide range of design and fabrication possibilites; marquetry, parquetry, custom veneering, inlay, relief and sculptural carving, decorative joinery, turning, and stained glass. Clarke's work is often characterized by strong geometric shapes, bold inlays, and graceful curves.

Clarke's architectural work has included kitchen's, wet bar's, offices, staircases, a wide range of built-in cabinetry, custom moldings, and furniture.

A high standard of quality and respect for budgetary and scheduling requirements is brought to every project. Prices for furniture range trom $1000.00 to $20,000.00.

(Above) Wet bar-cherry with stained glass and underlit glass tile counters. Architect: Jeff White. Photo: Scott Miles-Landmark Photography.

(Below) Armoire-curly koa, wengé, and mahogany. 90"H x 50"W x 22"D. Photo: David Levy.

Randy Cochran

Wood Studio
Route 3, Box 427
Decatur, AL 35603
(205) 350-5270

Working in a style he calls Southern contemporary, Randy Cochran designs furniture that is strongly influenced by his background in industrial design.

His works range from tables, chairs and case goods to commercial and residential cabinets.

Materials include solid hardwood, fine veneers, plastic laminates, metals and natural and synthetic stone.

Collaborative work is welcome. A brochure, photos, slides and references are available upon request.

(Top) Oak and leather rocker, 23"w x 42"h x 30"d, $2,000.

(Bottom) Left: Cherry side chair, 22"w x 44" h x 27"d, $1,000. Right: Yellow pine side chair with arms, 22"w x 44"h x 27"d, $1,100.

Prices do not include delivery.

Michael Colca
Michael O'Neal

SummerTree
711 Turtle Hill
Driftwood, TX 78619
(512) 847-5238,
Austin (512) 282-0493

SummerTree Partners, Michael Colca and Michael O'Neal, bring 25 years of experience to designing and crafting furniture of exceptional quality. The confluence of their ideas has brought forth "Medina", a selection with a uniquely Texas flair.

They work closely with interior designers, architectural firms and individuals. SummerTree welcomes residential and commercial projects in traditional and contemporary styling.

"Medina" Queen Size Bed in white oak; wenge accents. Full–$2,450, Queen–$2,495, King–$2,769.

"Medina" Side Table in white oak–$725, with shelf $825. Bed and Side Table available in other woods.

"Wishbone" Chair shown in walnut–$850 each (in sets of 4 or more).

Bench—Birdseye and hard rock maple; ebony accents. A custom design for bay window seating.

Showroom in Austin with Whit Hanks at Treaty Oak, 1009 W. 6th.

Culin Colella

Ray Culin
Janis Colella
632 Center Avenue
Mamaroneck, NY 10543
(914) 698-7727

(Bottom) Photographic Print Chest, By Janis Colella. 69" x 28" x 33". Bubinga and ebony.

(Top Left) Art Nouveau Fireplace Carving, By Janis Colella. 65" x 10" x 50". Curly Maple.

(Top Right) Writing Desk, By Ray Culin (Designed by Deborah Reiser). 60" x 24" x 29" Satin wood and ebony.

Photos: Rick Albert

Culin Colella

Ray Culin
Janis Colella
632 Center Avenue
Mamaroneck, NY 10543
(914) 698-7727

Ray Culin and Janis Colella bring together a special marriage of backgrounds in architecture, furniture design, sculpture, and woodworking.

Their distinctive blend of artistic flair and attention to detail has raised the combination of the fanciful and the practical to an artform. This is profoundly evident in their design and production of unique furniture, cabinetry, sculpture, architectural woodworking, and specialty finishing. Wide-ranging services, from design to fabrication, include one-of-a-kind and limited edition pieces, as well as contract furniture.

Works by Culin/Colella, which incorporate over thirty years of experience, are on display at Burlington House, Phillip Brothers, and Citicorp, and may be found in many fine homes and galleries in the tri-state area.

Details are available upon request.

(Top) Jan's Jewelry Box, By Ray Culin.

12" x 7 1/2" x 4". Curly maple, ebony, dyed maple, and polished lacquer.

(Bottom Right) Armoire, By Ray Culin. 30" x 24" x 90". Bird's eye maple, ebony and transparent polished lacquer.

(Bottom Left) Writing Desk, By Ray Culin (Designed by Deborah Reiser). 28" x 60" x 29". Curly maple, bird's eye maple and dyed veneer.

Photos: Rick Albert

Jeffrey Cooper

Designer of Sculptural Furnishings in Wood
135 McDonough Street
Portsmouth, NH 03801
(603) 436-7945

Art for Kids?

These chairs are lifetime treasures, ruggedly built, each handcarved with its own individuality. They are to be enjoyed by kids from 1 to 100!

Prices start at $1000. Commissions for any animal and portraits of special pets are welcome. Chairs measure 14 x 16 x 28H and a matching table is available to make a set

Animal chairs won the 1989 Stewart Nelson Award by ballot of the visitors at the Living with Craft Show, 56th annual League of NH Craftsmen's Fair.

Husky, Llama, Saddlehorse, Springbok (a type of gazelle), Giraffe

50

Glenn de Gruy

11630 Jeff Hamilton Road
Mobile, AL 36695
(205) 633-5765

Glenn de Gruy has been building custom furniture for 18 years. His training was in building authentic reproductions and restoring antique furniture using traditional hardwoods, cabinetmaking joinery and hand-rubbed lacquer finishes.

Currently, he uses mixed media and a variety of faux and painted finishes. Craft remains emphasized. The furniture is made to last for generations.

Pictured are two of de Gruy's designs for a boardroom setting. He also works to client specifications. De Gruy is often called on to build beds as well as a variety of other furniture. Prices upon request. Installation available.

(Top) The matching credenza, measuring 72"w x 30"h x 20"d, is solid mahogany with inlaid satinwood cross-banding.

(Bottom) Conference table measures 168"w x 30" h x 54"d. It has a satinwood field with Brazilian mahogany borders and base.

Jeremiah de Rham

de Rham Custom Furniture
43 Bradford Street
Concord, MA 01742
(508) 371-0353

Jeremiah de Rham specializes in the design and building of custom commission furniture for private clients and architects. From simple and elegant law office furniture to the fine art of carefully joined classic Chinese furniture, de Rham produces uncompromising quality of design and construction. All work is built with an eye to detail, from careful wood selection at the start through to the final, beautiful hand rubbed finish.

See work in Guild 5. Preliminary design fee of $100. Prices start near $1,000.

Commission prices dependent upon design and wood. Collaboration invited. Call for scheduling information.

(Top Right) Lawyer's office desk. Cherry. 30 1/2"h.x 40"w.x78"l.

(Top Left) Office side table. Cherry. 28"h.x 20 1/2"w.x56"l.

(Bottom) Coffee table. East Indian rosewood. Single board panel top. 17"h.x21"w.x52"l.

Peter S. Dean

465-D Medford Street
Charlestown, MA 02129
(617) 242-2536

Peter Dean designs and builds one-of-a-kind and limited edition fine furniture for the residential and corporate market. The designs range from conference tables and corporate offices to individual pieces designed specifically for clients' homes.

Direct contact with clients and collaboration with architects, designers and other artists are welcome.

Existing designs can be adapted in terms of size, materials and function, or entirely new designs may be commissioned.

Prices start at $3,000; F.O.B. Charlestown, MA.

Slides and resumé available upon request.

Mandala table, 42" diameter x 5 ½" h, birdseye maple, ebony and glass, $5,800

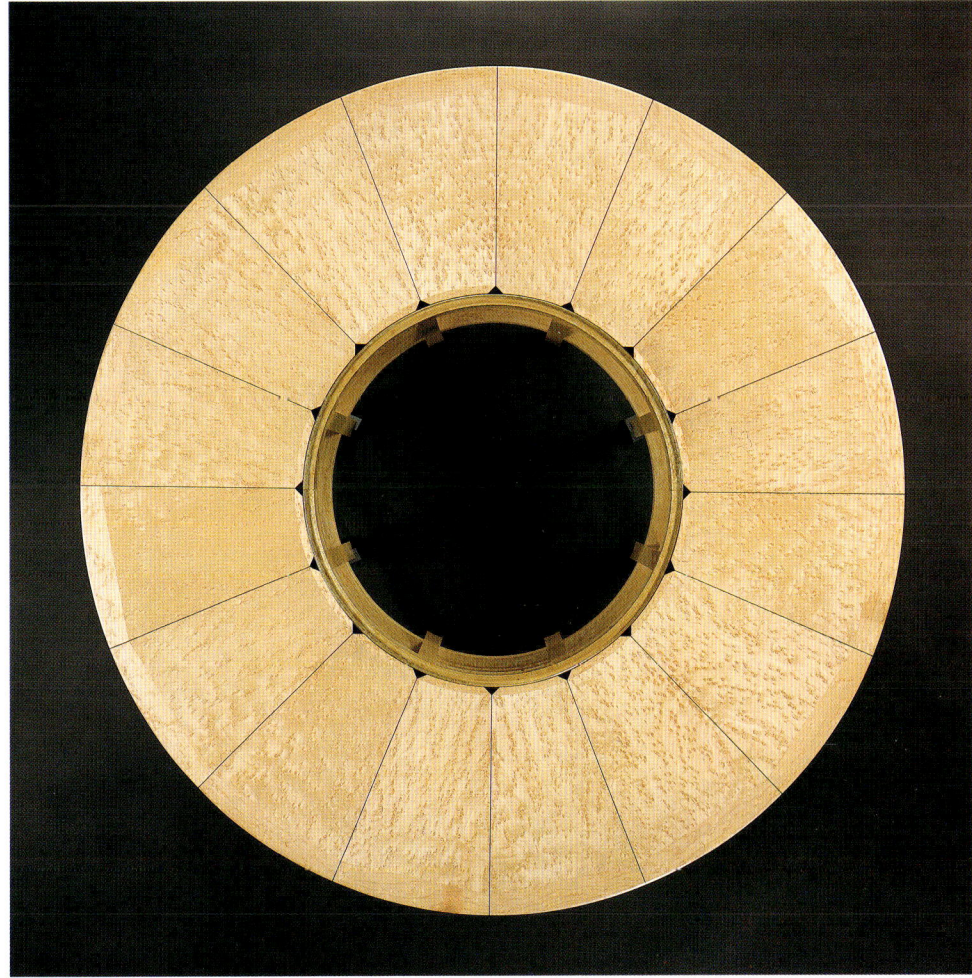

Ron Diefenbacher

Ron Diefenbacher Designs
12132 Big Bend
St Louis, MO 63122
(314) 966-4829

From design to delivery, Ron Diefenbacher uses a professional approach in assessing clients' needs and developing creative solutions. Combining artistic skill and an ability to work well with architects, interior designers, and private parties, Diefenbacher creates signature pieces which stress the individuality of each new project. These unique designs are placed in many private collections, executive offices, and fine galleries across the country.

Diefenbacher has a Master of Arts in Furniture Design and teaches Woodworking and Furniture Design at Washington University in St. Louis.

(Bottom left) Pescadero Lamp: teak, ebony, copper.

(Bottom right) Detail, Pescadero Lamp.

(Top right) Writing Desk: padauk.

Ron Diefenbacher

Ron Diefenbacher Designs
12132 Big Bend
St. Louis, MO 63122
(314) 966-4829

Design fees, slide portfolio, references and
prices available upon request.

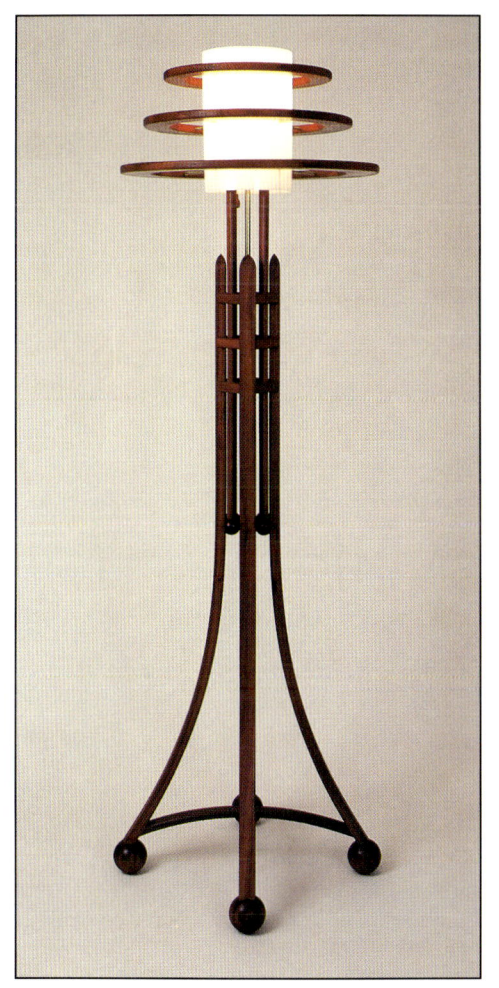

John Dodd

John Dodd Studio
1237 East Main Street
Rochester, NY 14609
(716) 482-7233

John Dodd has maintained a successful furniture studio for the past twelve years. A graduate of the School for American Craftsmen, he has won numerous awards including artists' fellowships from the New York Foundation for the Arts in 1985 and 1989. His work has been exhibited in the American Craft Museum and other museums and galleries throughout the United States.

The current series of screens is designed to complement residential or commercial interiors with potential as room dividers, foyer or lobby pieces. Custom design makes possible the inclusion of elements such as display cabinets, shelves or table surfaces.

A rendering or model with firm price and completion date are provided upon receipt of a 10% design fee. Average time from design to installation is four months.

Slides and pricing information available upon request.

Thomas J. Duffy

Duffy's General & Specific Millwork
52 E. River Street
Ogdensburg, NY 13669
(315) 393-8553
Fax (315) 393-4827

Studio crafts are alive, well and available from Tom Duffy. From one-of-a-kind designs and fabrications to collaborations with other crafts artist, promise is made good.

Duffy's range of work is from design/build furniture to unusual architectural woodworking and boat building (see Architectural Wood page).

More information upon request.

(Clockwise) Bench: Holly veneer, English Harewood, purplehearts—dyed wood, inlays and gold leaf, 14½" x 16½" x 34".
Collection: Boston Museum of Fine Arts, 1985.

Pentimento™: Folding Screen, 76" x 76", drop matched Holly with dyed wood inlays, curly maple frame, 1987.

Detail: Inlay—dyed woods in Holly Veneer, 1990.

Chair Within A Chair: Pentimento™, 23" x 29" x 39". Drop matched Holly dyed wood inlay, 1990.

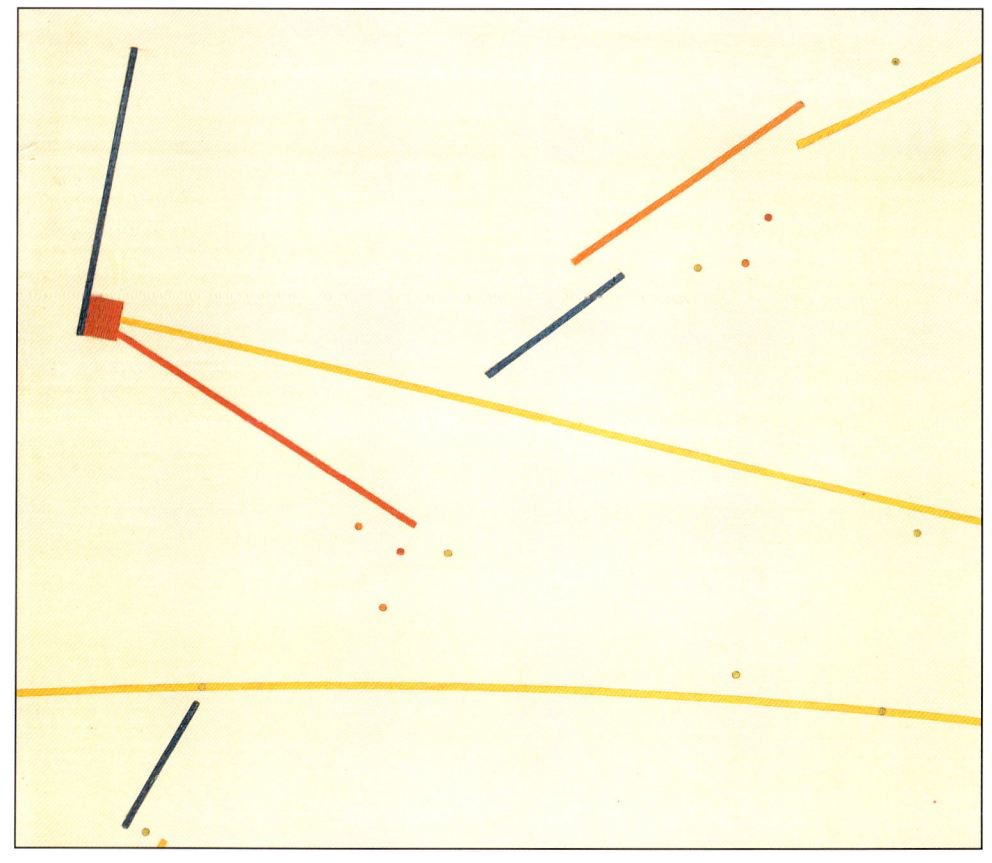

Kevin Earley

1231 E. Wilson Street
Madison, WI 53703
(608) 256-5171

For twenty years Kevin Earley has designed and built furniture which blends the practical with the beautiful. He combines wood and veneers, metal, glass, stone and fabric to meet the individual demands of residential and business clients.

Innovative use of inlay is a hallmark of his work.

Prices begin at $2,000 with delivery time from two to six months.

(Clockwise) Sofa d'Amore—cherry, inlay, wool upholstery 77w. x 31h. x 28d.
Detail of d'Amore.
Hat Cabinet—Cypress & ebony, oil and paste wax finish 22w. x 65h. x 16d.
Sideboard—Walnut, dyed inlay, gold leaf, catalyzed varnish finish—42w. x 50h. x 21d.
Photos: Lois Stauber.

Michael Elkan

Michael Elkan Studio
22364 N. Fork Road
Silverton, OR 97381
(503) 873-3241

Michael Elkan lives in the foothills of Oregon's Cascade Mountains. Surrounded by the trees from which he draws his inspiration, each sculpted object is made from a single piece of wood. Slowly air dried, much like musical instrument wood—whole dining sets can be made from a single tree.

Elkan's designs harmonize with the natural structure of the tree and show a deep understanding of human form as well; dining and rocking chair spindles canted at a variety of compound angles to fit the back; chair seats deeply contoured for extra comfort. Highly figured, collectable quality, native and exotic woods are his specialty.

(Above) "Slat work desk" Highly figured curly maple, 5 drawers.

(Below) "Accordian base table" 84" x 42"—spring quilted Oregon maple burl, with 8 matching chairs.

Michael Emmons

Laughing Willows
Partington Ridge
Big Sur, CA 93920
(408) 667-2133

Michael Emmons designs and builds furniture with the focus on bringing the essence of nature into the living space. Using the hardwoods of the California coast, he works primarily with eucalyptus, for its expressive character and silky surface texture.

He works with interior and restaurant designers, as well as individual clients, and will build pieces for specific situations. Upholstery available: leather, handpainted canvas, and cuttings from Turkish kilims. Emmons' work has been featured in Metropolitan Home, House Beautiful, N.Y. Times Home Magazine, Elle Décor, and Town and Country.

Prices start at around $600.

Catalog available: $3.00.

Frank Garvelink

52558 Burlington Road
Marcellus, MI 49067
(616) 646-9055

Frank Garvelink specializes in heirloom quality rocking chairs, handcrafted from solid walnut and cherry for individual and corporate collections.

Garvelink's designs harmonize the natural structure and grain of the wood with the natural structure of the human form. Curved spindles to fit the back, chair seats deeply contoured for comfort, laminated runners with brakes, all insure beauty and comfort.

(Top) High Back Rocker Cherry, Soft Maple 48"h.x28 1/2"w.x41"l. Price range $1600–$2000.

(Lower) Bow Back Rocker Black Walnut, Soft Maple 37"h.x24"w.x36"l. Price range $1300–$1500.

Delivery Time is 3–6 months.

Brad Greenwood

Greenwood Designs
13624 Idaho-Maryland Road
Nevada City, CA 95959
(916) 273-8183

Brad Greenwood combines natural form and function in furniture that has rustic character and simplistic style. The materials are primarily oak branches, complemented by other fine woods.

He designs and crafts a complete line of furniture, beginning with selection and cutting of trees and stripping of bark. Instead of nails and screws, mortise-and-tenon joints and carved pegs solidly unite the wood. The smooth, hand-sanded finish distinguishes

Greenwood furniture from other works of similar style.

Strength, comfort and quality are incorporated into each unique design, and every piece is signed and numbered.

Greenwood has participated in a number of custom projects and considers specific requirements in each commission. Delivery time is eight weeks or more. For additional information, please contact the studio.

John Hein

87 Woodland Avenue
Trenton, NJ 08638
(609) 883-4573

John Hein's wood furniture contains a blend of traditional and contemporary aesthetics. A traditional respect for nature and purity of craftsmanship combined with a contemporary structure are the aesthetic principles influencing their design and construction. Furniture is joined with mortise-and-tenon and dovetail joints, and instead of screws to reinforce crucial joints, carved pegs are used. Hein chooses woods containing suggestive patterns, woods he combines to create warm and subtle furniture, furniture with gentle surfaces and elegant lines. Most pieces cost between $2,000 and $9,000 depending on size, number of drawers, and complexity of design.

(Top) "Side Table" of cocobolo, American black walnut, and Ceylon satinwood (32" x 42" x 14").

(Bottom) "Spalted Maple Door Cabinet" of maple, East Indian rosewood, and walnut (66" x 13" x 10").

William Hewitt

Witticks Design
46 River Road, RFD
South Deerfield, MA 01373
(413) 527-5973

William Hewitt has run a custom furniture and cabinet shop for the last eight years. His work has generally involved pieces designed to fit into existing spaces while expressing his own solution. His work emphasizes the use of solid wood construction and woods of contrasting colors.

William is accustomed to collaborating with clients concerning ideas and due dates. He will provide drawings for projects of major scale for a design fee, while bids are supplied free of charge.

Steven Holman

P.O. Box 572
Dorset, VT 05251
(802) 867-0131

Steven Holman's designs combine a respect for the past with an enthusiasm for the future. All work is crafted to the highest standards and manifests meticulous attention to detail. He has maintained a studio over a decade. Mr. Holman has collaborated with architects and interior designers on residential and corporate commissions, as well as provided quality installation services. A firm price and delivery estimate are established for each commission, most of which can be executed within sixteen weeks.

Slides, resume, and pricing information available upon request.

(Bottom left) Corner cabinet: bubinga, oak, maple, rosewood, black lacquer; 22"d x 34" w x 84"h.

(Top right) Temple table: cherry, curly, maple, wenge; 18"h x 27"w x 44"l.

(Bottom right) Coffee table: curly oak, padauk; 17"h x 22 "w x 40"l.

Ian Ingersoll

Ian Ingersoll Cabinetmakers
Main Street
West Cornwall, CT 06796
(203) 672-6334

Specializing in Shaker furniture and reproductions. Ian Ingersoll works in Northwestern Connecticut where he maintains a showroom displaying 20 to 30 pieces.

Commissions for the production of any Shaker design are accepted.

A catalog of chair designs is available for $5.

(Right) Shaker arm chair, $425.

(Below) #5 Shaker side chairs, $385 each.

Bob Ingram

Ingram Design Studio
1102 East Columbia Avenue
Philadelphia, PA 19125
(215) 739-7253

Ingram Design Studio designs, develops, fabricates and/or markets furniture for designer showrooms, gallery sales and commercial manufacture. These designs are also adapted to the individual needs of a private office, an executive boardroom or a fine residence.

Commissions are completed in 6–16 weeks. The work of Ingram Design Studio is available directly or through Dennis Miller Associates, New York City; The Works Gallery, Philadelphia.

Slides, resume and further information are available upon request.

Centennial hall table. Kathy Halton, co-designer.

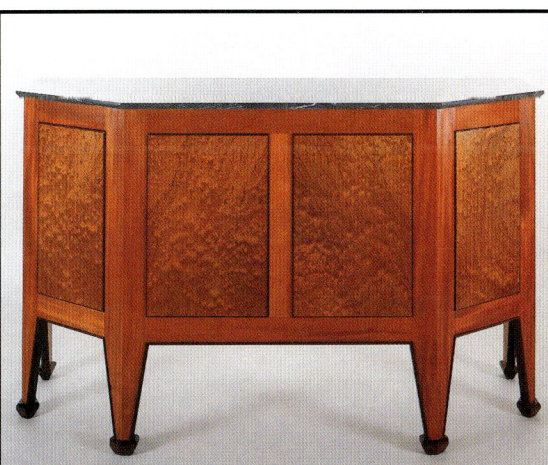

Folson sideboard, available in various sizes and as High Boy.

Autumn light blanket chest. Kathy Halton, co-designer.

Folson settee, available as 1, 2 or 3 seater.

Post and bracket dining table.

Ira A. Keer, AIA

P.O. Box 50115
Minneapolis, MN 55405
(612) 871-8802

Ira Keer's whimsical furniture is designed to be used. With each piece he aims to elicit an emotion, enticing the beholder into its matrix of concept, craftsmanship and utility.

Keer's furniture designs inject fantasy and playfulness into ageless architectonic elements and period styles. His conceptual furniture ideas now emerging in three dimensions, have been exhibited in select galleries and museums. His work is recognized in a wide range of publications and has won numerous design awards.

A practicing architect, Keer's designs are executed by a spirited collaboration with select Minnesota craftsmen. This collaboration ensures excellence of design as well as the finest construction, materials and finishes.

He produces both one-of-a-kind pieces and limited edition works. Special orders, collaborations and commissions are encouraged. More information, brochure upon request.

T. SQUARES: An Armoire ©1988. Curly maple, brazil and ebonized walnut; 73 1/2"h x 34"W x 22 1/2"D; Fabrication, Bruce Kieffer; Photography, Bill Zuehlke.

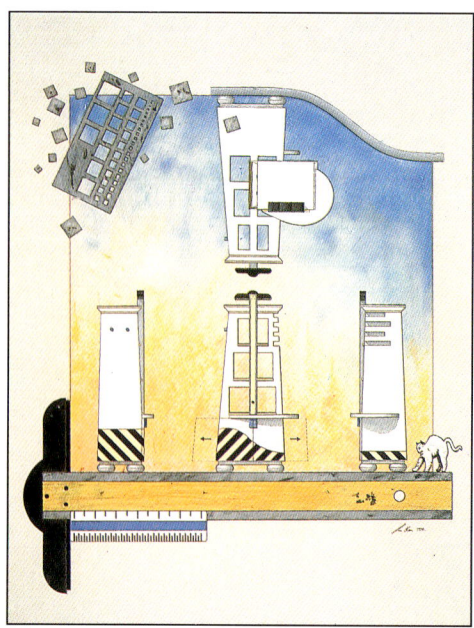

Ira A. Keer
P. O. Box 50115
Minneapolis, MN 55405
(612) 871-8802

DAPHY: A Winged Armchair © 1986. Duck-like features characterize this whimsical rendition of a classic.
Birdseye and curly maple, ebony stained walnut and mahogany. 41½"h x 43½"w x 32"d
Fabrication, Bruce Kieffer; Photography, Steven Greenway.

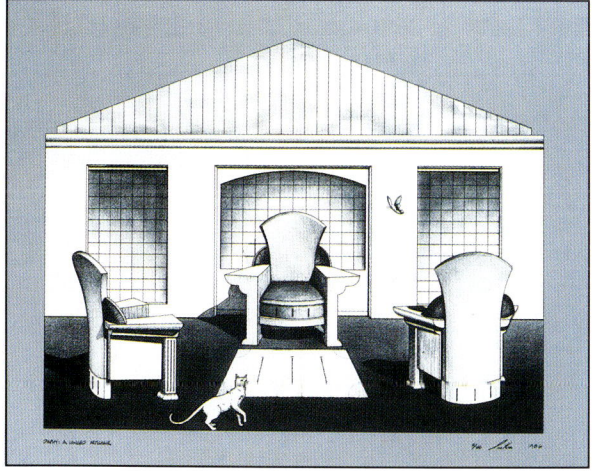

Darryl Keil

Darryl Keil, Ltd.
10A South St.
Freeport, ME 04032
(207) 865-6318

Darryl Keil's Limited Edition furniture presents elegant functional art forms hand-crafted from unique woods selected for color, grain, and figure. Each piece is available in a variety of these woods which can be personally selected. The line has evolved over 15 years as a designer and craftsman of custom, commissioned work in wood. Prices and slides of additional designs available upon request.

(Top right) Round dining table, bleached maple butt, ebonized maple and black marble center, 60" dia. x 29"h.

(Top left) Writing table of ebonized maple and curly koa. 36" x 72" x 29"h.

(Bottom) Credenza, tineo and ebonized maple, 18" x 69" x 32"h.

Monte Lindsley

Ptarmigan Willow
P.O. Box 551
Fall City, WA 98024
(206) 392-5767

Monte Lindsley has been designing contemporary willow furniture since 1978. His work has been shown nationally and featured in magazines and newspapers.

Educated as a landscape designer and a forester, he incorporates his love of plants and nature into his work.

His works are constructed in limited individual editions. All his materials are native to the Northwest. Monte personally hand selects, gathers and prepares his materials.

One of Monte's goals is to create a more eloquent contemporary look to a traditional craft form. This he achieves through his flowing loop designs and use of specially selected materials. His work consists of bark, peeled and color finishes.

Contact the artist for a brochure. Delivery time runs 4–6 months.

(Top left) Peeled willow mountain forest bed.

(Bottom left) Peeled willow dining set.

(Top right) Peeled willow bed.

(Center right) Bark willow headboard.

(Bottom right) Peeled willow gazebo bed.

Gregg Lipton

Furniture Design
1 Mill Ridge Road
Cumberland, ME 04012
(207) 829-5010

Gregg Lipton's furniture reflects his sensitivity to the relationship between user and environment, it is this aesthetic sensitivity that won him a national merit award for his design and craftsmanship in 1988.

Prices start at $600. Orders are filled within 10–16 weeks. Collaborative as well as commission work is welcome.

Catalog and price list available for $5 upon request.

(Top left and right) "Roxy", coffee table and bench, 60"w x 17"h x 18"d. Rosewood, Swiss pearwood.

(Bottom left) Side and arm chairs for dining or occasional seating, 22"w x 42"h x 21"d, cherry. Torchere, 75"h, cherry and holly.

(Center right) Bench, 37"w x 18"h x 14"d. Pickled ash. The design is easily adapted to accommodate one to 10 sculpted seats.

(Bottom right) Diningroom set. "Bridge" table is made to accommodate any size glass. Side chairs are sold separately as a settee.

Jeffry Mann

P.O. Box 3420
Aspen, CO 81611
(303) 925-8651

Jeffry Mann designs furniture using selected, dramatic wood from around the world. His pieces are sculptured and functional. Each is a delight to the eye, the hand, and the body as it is experienced visually, tactilely and kinesthetically.

He is known for his rocking chairs but welcomes inquiries on commissions of all kinds. Rocking chairs range in price from $2,500 to $4,000, according to materials and design. Commissions require from 3 to 12 months.

Peter Maynard

Peter Maynard and Associates
P.O. Box 77, Main Street
South Acworth, NH 03607
(603) 835-2969

As a master furnituremaker, Peter Maynard offers excellence in design in a broad range of styles. He has evolved his own aesthetic statement with Classical Chinese, Native American, European and other influences.

For eighteen years he has worked with both designers and private individuals to create fine furniture and architectural installations.

Prices and photos of additional designs are available upon request.

Card table, closed.

Card table, solid curly maple with ebony and rosewood inlays. 30"h.x36"l.x18"d. (36"d. when opened)

Drafting table, tilt mechanism.

Drafting table, painted bases with red oak top and base detail. Dimensions vary according to clients' requirements. $1950.

Loy Davis Martin

Loy D. Martin Furniture
3300-A Park Boulevard
Palo Alto, CA 94306
(415) 856-2834

Every design from Loy D. Martin answers to the individual environment and needs of the client. The result is an unusual range of stylistic expression and technique. Trained in aesthetics and the history of furniture styles, Loy Martin has shown in major west coast galleries and in national publications like American Craft and Design Book Four. Some pieces are frankly contemporary while others make allusions to design vocabularies of different eras. Richness and rarity of materials and the highest standards of workmanship characterize each piece.

John McAlevey

John McAlevey Woodworking Studio
Mill Street
Warner, NH 03278
(603) 456-2135

John McAlevey designs and builds fine furniture in his studio in Warner, NH. His furniture is made from domestic and imported hardwoods. A variety of finishes are available and while John usually prefers an oil finish, he will help you choose one appropriate to your requirements.

John McAlevey draws upon an extensive knowledge of woodworking design and traditional joinery to convey strength of line and attention to detail in his work.

Residential and corporate commissions are accepted. The time from initial contact to delivery is 3–6 months, depending on the size of the commission.

Design portfolio $3.00.

Blanket chest ebonized mahogany, 16"h x 26" x 16".

Folding screen left, cherry, right, walnut, 66"h x 56"l.

Thomas Moser

Thos. Moser Cabinetmakers, Inc.
415CC Cumberland Avenue
Portland, ME 04101
(207) 774-3791

Thos. Moser Cabinetmakers produces hand-crafted standard and custom designs for corporate, library and residential use. Known for their integrity in construction, commitment to utility and reverence for wood, their designs are gracefully proportioned interpretations of classic American furniture. Theywork predominately in solid cherry, hand selected for its distinctive color and clarity of grain. All surfaces are finished with linseed oil and wax and polished to a satin sheen to encourage the natural patino.

Awards include Daphnes in 1984 and 1985, and the IBD Gold in 1984 and 1986.

Thos. Moser has showrooms in Philadelphia, Portland, ME and Alexandria, VA.

A list of contract representatives for the architectural and design community available upon request.

Catalog of residential designs: $9.00

Andrew Pate Design

Box 199A, RD 3
Greenwich, NY 12834
(518) 692-7676

Andrew Pate and Ray Mullineaux design and build fine furniture, cabinetry, and architectural wood work.

They welcome inquiries from architects, designers and collectors; and encourage active participation of clients in the design process.

Attention to detail, material selection, and the tradition of high quality craftsmenship in wood are hall marks of their work.

Professional services include design consultation, production, contracting and installation.

(Right) Shaker cupboard, 45" tall, painted pine, $3900.

(Below) Oval Bar, 40" tall, curly red oak, birdseye maple, pink marble, $10,500.

Ronald C. Puckett

Ronald C. Puckett & Company
P.O. Box 9549
Richmond, VA 23228
(804) 752-2126

"Ron uses the colors of wood to define the forms and shapes of his furniture, like a painter uses color, creating elegant, fluid, and regal furniture."

Veena Singh
Gallery owner
Sansar Gallery
Washington, D.C.

Ron Puckett is available for both corporate and residential commissions. His furniture can be seen in interior architect Patricia Conway's *Art for Everyday*, the *Guild 4 & 5* as well as galleries in Washington, D.C., Philadelphia, Pa. and East Hampton, N.Y. Recent corporate commissions include Southern Progress Corporation, Birmingham, Alabama, and the MONY headquarters in New York. Ron was a Merit Winner in the Kraus-Sikes 3rd American Crafts Awards. Photos of current works are available from the artist.

(Top)"Night Moves Desk," detail, leather, padouk, wenge, maple, 29"h X 72"w x 36"d.

(Bottom right) "Night Moves Desk," padouk, wenge, maple, leather, 29"h x 72"W x36"d.

(Bottom left) "Metropolis Chair," bubinga, wenge, leather, 35"h x 34"w x 32"d.

Ronald C. Puckett

Ronald C. Puckett & Company
P.O. Box 9549
Richmond, VA 23228
(804) 752-2126

(Clockwise) "Lap of Luxury," mahogany, fiddleback mahogany, wenge, fabric, 34"h x 66"w x 32"d.

"Atlas Table," bubinga, wenge, 28"h x 28"d.

"Pawling Cabinet," figured maple, cherry, wenge, padouk, slate, 56"h x 42"w x 24"d.

"Bow Front," bubinga, wenge, 34"h x 56"w x 20"d.

Marcy Pesner

Beagle Tiles
300 8th Avenue, #3E
Brooklyn, NY 11215
(718) 965-3654

The piece on the right entitled "Saratoga Beagle" is a kitchen pantry complete with slamming screen door and interior bug light.

Every piece comes with a Beagle Tile inlay custom coloured to the clients' specifications.

Beagle Tiles are the only wooden tiles on the market and come in squares, rectangles, and triangles to create a myriad of mosaic configurations.

Bert Ray

2472 Bolsover, Suite 345
Houston, TX 77005
(713) 528-5062

As an architect, Bert Ray approaches the art of wood inlay as rich patterning to enhance an environment.

Utilizing nature's magnificent palette of natural wood colors and textures (no stains), he creates one-of-a-kind surfaces. These may be purchased as panels only, or finished pieces such as tables, screens or headboards.

The work is a personal interpretation of age old techniques of wood inlay, marquetry and tunbridgeware. Each surface is meticulously crafted with veneers created by hand by the artist—as many as 4,000 pieces per square foot. Accents of semiprecious stones or metals may be included.

Collaboration to accommodate client themes or motifs is acceptable.

Prices and schedules upon request.

Jamie Robertson

Jamie Robertson Designs
43 Bradford Street
W. Concord, MA 01742
(508) 371-1106

For the past 17 years Jamie Robertson has been designing and building one-of-a-kind and limited edition furniture which draws on both classical and contemporary references.

A master of traditional techniques, he has also created several of his own. Many of Robertson's pieces feature decorative inlay and marquetry, and each piece is uniquely designed for its environment.

Robertson's designs and superb craftsmanship have won him awards and international acclaim, including articles in magazines such as *House and Garden* and *Architectural Record*.

Slides, resumé and prices upon request.

(Top Left) Lunette end tables, 24"w x 26"h x 16"d.

(Bottom left) Blue and white table, 48"w x 30"h x 21"d.

(Top right) Hall cabinet, 40"w x 40"h x 18"d.

(Bottom right) High back chair, 19"w x 52"h x 18"d.

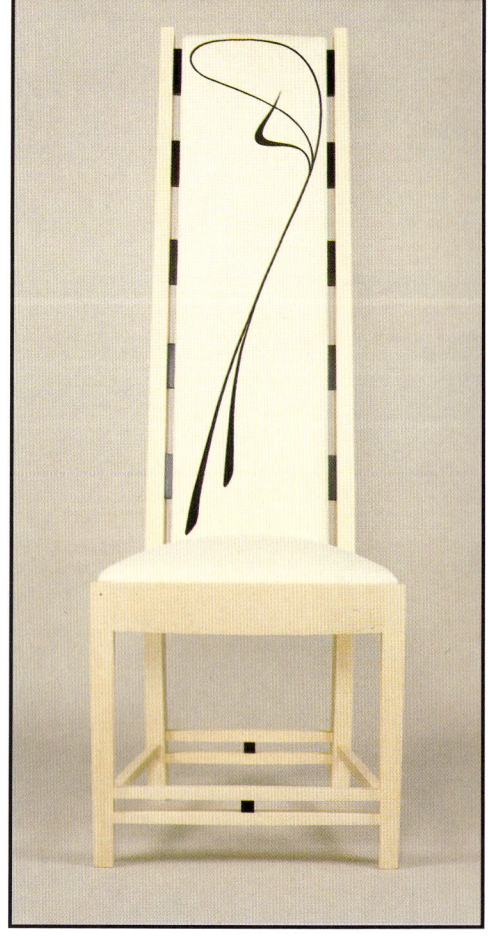

Anne Shutan

RR 1 Box 991
Newfane, VT 05345
(802) 365-7118

Anne Shutan creates one-of-a-kind pieces of furniture and sculpture affirming the sensuous nature of wood. Through her work, she has discovered that art has as much to do with finesse and taking chances as with intelligence and craft. Shutan travels all over the country to discuss projects with her clients. She then returns to her studio to design and create the piece. The process from conception to delivery takes from one to six months. Shutan accepts commissions for both interior and outdoor pieces.

Please contact artist for information regarding commissions.

A portfolio is available upon request.
Sculpture $500–$10,000
Furniture $2,000–$10,000

(Below) Walnut table, 30"w x 40"l x 30"h

(Right) Rosewood sculpture, 24"w x 30"h

Wm. B. Sayre, Inc.

One Cottage Street
Easthampton, MA 01027
(413) 527-0202
(413) 527-0502 Fax

Fine commissioned furniture executed to the designs of specifying architect, interior designer, or residential customer.

Working in the finest hardwoods available, collaborating in a wide range of other media to produce heirlooms of distinction and innovation.

Full design services available. Complete production facilities.

Brochure available upon request.

Australian lacewood, zinc etching plate, bevelled glass.

William B. Sayre

Wm. B. Sayre, Inc.
One Cottage Street
Easthampton, MA 01027
(413) 527-0202
(413) 527-0502 Fax

© 1989 Wm. B. Sayre, Inc. Jatoba. Designed by Wm. Sayre.

Leather on-lay in Nigerian goat leather.

Kathran Siegel

3311 San Jose Boulevard
Jacksonville, FL 32207
(904) 396-6325

Visually playful, the furnishings of Kathran Siegel interact with their environment as sculpture without sacrificing function.

Each work is carved from laminated hardwoods and protected with a water and alcohol resistant lacquer finish, making it durable for indoor use.

Large pieces break down for crating and shipping. These easy-to-assemble sculptural furnishings are limited editions or custom designed.

Educated as a painter, for the past 20 years Siegel has applied her primary interest in color to her work in wood. She exhibits nationally and internationally and is represented in several museum collections.

(Top and bottom) Another view of Mount Fuji, Matisse Modern Series, birch and acrylic. Lacquer Finish Bed: 42"w x 38"h x 83"l. Nightstand: 14"w x 22"h x 7"d.

Brad Smith

Bradford Woodworking
3120 Fisher Road Box 157
Worcester, PA. 19490
(215) 584-1150

Bradford Woodworking was established in 1980 by Brad Smith upon graduating from the School for American Craftsmen at Rochester Institute of Technology.

Brad has concentrated on a line of stools and chairs which are characterized by legs resembling ax handles. These legs are made on an 1850's vintage ax handle lathe which he has modified to suit his needs and to create unusual spiraling surface textures.

Average delivery time is 4 weeks. More information available upon request.

(Top Left) Ax Handle Stools. Five heights 18"–30" with or without backs. Retail price range $110.–210.

(Top Right) Fork Chairs. 18" high at seat front. 31" over-all height. $240.

(Bottom) Farm Series Tables. One of a kind pieces.

Price range $500.–1000.

Bill Stankus

611 Bradford Parkway
DeWitt, NY 13224
(315) 446-6761

Bill Stankus is an American craftsman whose designs are imbued with the beauty and strength of the best traditional joinery. Disdaining mass-production techniques, Stankus works with an intuitive understanding which transfigures the original materials.

Unique traditional and contemporary pieces are executed in the finest manner and enriched by his ideals and reverence. Ever cognizant, his client's personality and preferences are always given the utmost consideration.

Prices begin under $1,000. Most orders can be met within eight weeks after design approval.

For more information, contact Bill at his workshop.

(Top) End tables, walnut; bowl, mahogany, oak, walnut.

(Bottom left) Chair, walnut, zebrawood.

(Bottom right) Game table with reversible top, walnut, ebony, maple.

Thomas W. Stender

9339 Boston State Road
Boston, NY 14025
(716) 941-6388

Thomas W. Stender makes one-of-a-kind and limited edition hardwood furniture. Distinguished by their sensual and lyrical forms as well as by their gestural qualities, his award-winning designs have been exhibited nationwide. He collaborates with architects and interior designers to furnish specific environments.

Prices begin about $1,000.

Price list and current slides available on request.

(Top) "Wave Goodbye," hall table, curly maple and cherry, 12½"w x 61"l x 31½"h, edition limited to one hundred.

(Bottom) "Canilune" chair, padouk, birdseye maple, lacewood, 52½"h, edition limited to two hundred.

David Stenstrom

45 Park Street
Portland, ME 04101
(207) 772-7643
(207) 774-9298

David Stenstrom makes custom furniture inspired by the strong, sophisticated designs and character of 17th and 18th Century American country furniture. He uses traditional construction, mostly native woods, and sometimes paint to make pieces that are friendly and easy to live with. He would like to work with your design ideas and requirements. His shop is capable of small production runs. Price quotes are available on request. The usual delivery time is 2 to 6 months but he will try to accommodate your schedule.

Pencil post bed—maple and red lacquer,

Desk—antique Southern yellow pine,

Owls eye chair—ebonized mahogany and paint,

Pilgrim chest—oak and paint.

Edward Wohl

Edward S. Wohl Woodworking & Design
Route 1
Ridgeway, WI 53582
(608) 924-9411

Ed Wohl and wood chose each other. He, perhaps, was reassured by its abundance: that he would run out before it did. Maybe the wood saw the opposite in Ed: a chance for lending itself to a level of artisanship fast approaching extinction. The results are neither exclusively art nor craft. They are wholly wood and Wohl.

Wohl creates one-of-a-kind and limited production pieces on commission for residential and corporate use. Expect delightful design, meticulous joinery, innovative solutions to functional challenges and deep, liquid-smooth finishes—even in the hidden parts you'll never see or touch.

(Top left and bottom right) Bowfront collector's cabinet in walnut with interchangeable drawers, 26"w x 36"h x 20"d.

(Top right) Highchair in cherry with removable tray.

(Bottom left) Rocking chair in birdseye maple.

FURNITURE IN MIXED MEDIA 2

Modern Objects

Michael Aguero
Michael Sarti
18 Marshall Street
South Norwalk, CT 06854
866-0334   Fax 866-9469

Their cumulative knowledge and experience in all phases of design have had innovative results for Michael Aguero and Michael Sarti with the introduction of Modern Objects an affordable addition to the parts furniture and home accessories market.

Their criteria are pure use of materials, simple design and engineering, beauty and strength. The choice of materials such as wood, glass, steel and marble is derived from an architectural aesthetic. They are crafted so that the natural beauty and textures are enhanced and then combined with such elements as unusual patinaes, exotic papers, leather hinges and natural fibers.

Their initial concept of designing a line of products inspired by architectural form has established this team as a major contributing force to a trend that has become the strongest influence in the design of home furnishings today. A brochure is available upon request.

Chris Axelsson

Axelsson Metalsmith
P.O. Box 22-2598
Carmel; CA 93922
Phone: (408) 624-3909
Fax: (408) 624-3579

Fine metalworking skills have been achieved to offer the highest standards in reviving period ironwork and fashioning contemporary designs. Chris Axelsson's work is hand-forged and lends an organic quality to materials such as iron, copper and bronze.

Honored with numerous gold medals from the National Ornamental Metals Association, the artist's private and corporate commissions include sculpture, lighting, gates and furniture. A line of fine furnishings is offered in the form of tables, beds, lamps, candleabras and fireplace implements. Axelsson is accustomed to working closely with architects, owners and design firms. Installation is available nationwide. A design and production period is required for major commissions.

Inquiries are welcomed.

Pictured is a California King Iron Bed. Forged and fabricated mild steel, with quartz crystal.

Eric W. Bergman

Neophlle Inc.
1239 Broadway
NYC, NY 10001
(212) 925-4956

Eric Bergman started Neophlle in 1984. The studio produces a comprehensive line of furniture, lighting and decorative accessories. All of the pieces are hand-made and hand-painted. Glass designs are cut and sand-blasted in-house.

Custom colors are available on most pieces. Commissions for residential and commercial installations as well as display and special events props are welcomed.

Brochure and price list available upon request.

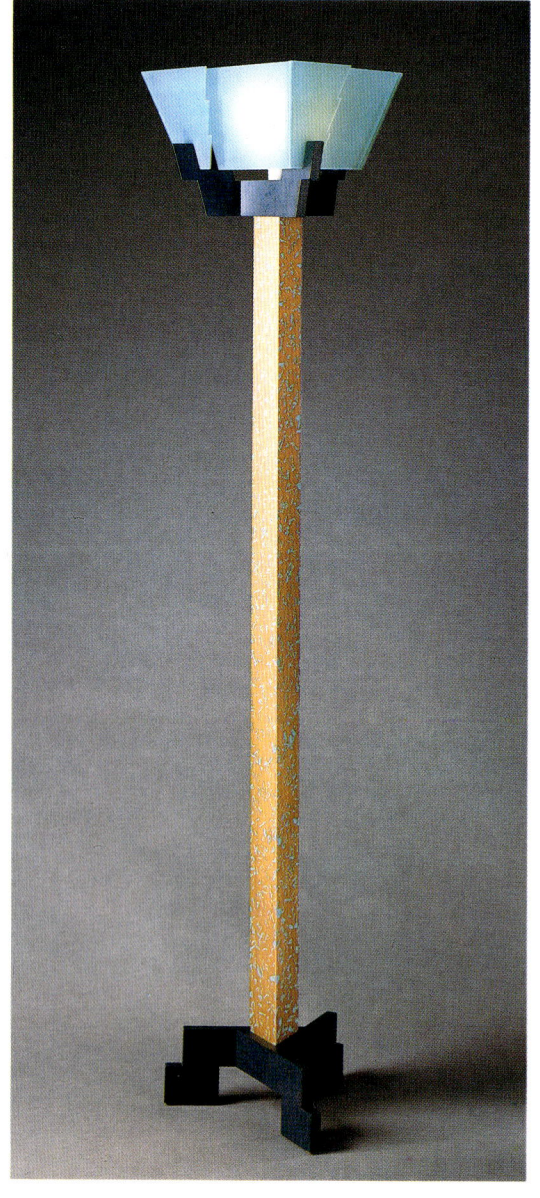

Warren Carther

Warren Carther Glass Studio
223 Roslyn Road
Winnipeg, Manitoba
Canada R3LOH5
(204) 453-2496

Warren Carther received his glass education studying with Bill Carlson in New York and later under Marvin Lipofsky at C.C.A.C. in California (B.F.A. 1978). He has been creating architectural and sculptural glass for 16 yrs., often collaborating with architects and designers.

His attention is now turning to carved glass tables, both as limited editions and unique pieces. Price range: $10,000.–$20,000.

Carther's technique is to fire on color and to carve deeply with abrasive blast into very thick, sometimes laminated glass.

The artist's work is found across Canada, parts of the U.S., Europe and Japan. At this printing he is producing a mullionless carved glass wall 25'hx20' for the new Canadian embassy in Tokyo.

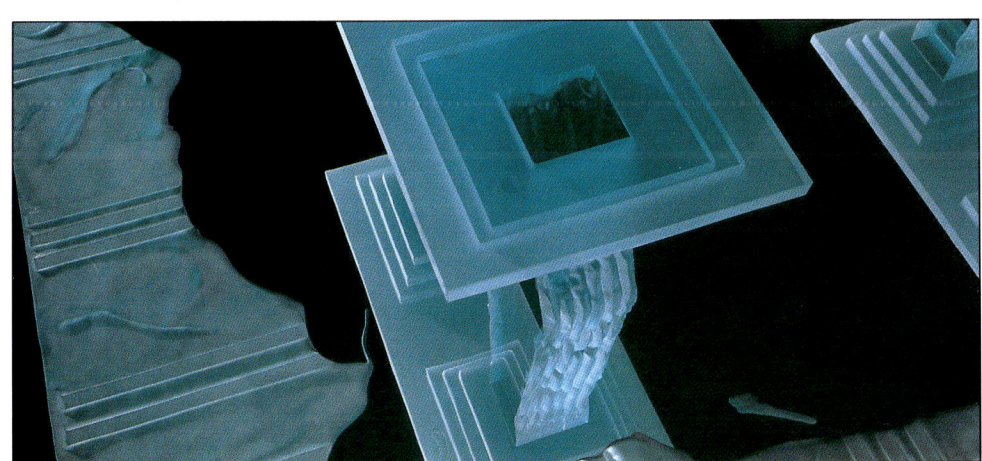

Detail: Laminated and carved table.

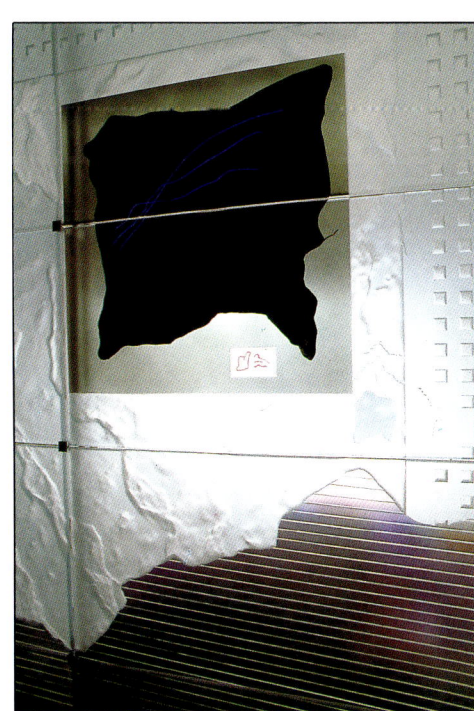

Detail: Mullionless carved glass wall 90" x 78" x ¾"

Laminated and carved glass table, 120" x 54" x 29"h, weight 1500 lb.

rear photo showing Mullionless support 90" x 78" x ¾".

Robert L. Crecelius

St. Francois Forge
Route 5 Box 5198
Farmington, MO 63640
(314) 756-1201

Robert Crecelius has been forging iron as a blacksmith for over ten years. Specializing in interior pieces, Crecelius creates furniture and lighting in both traditional and contemporary designs, as well as fireplace accessories and decorative screens and grillwork.

St. Francois Forge is familiar in working with blueprints and can provide scaled working drawings of projects for a retainer fee.

Crecelius is willing to collaborate on specific projects and has done so in the past. Prices vary in range depending on complexity of design and installation if required. Iron and glass table, lower right $800.

Further information available upon request.

Peter S. Dean

465-D Medford Street
Charlestown, MA 02129
(617) 242-2536

Peter Dean designs and builds one-of-a-kind and limited edition fine furniture for the residential and corporate market. The designs range from conference tables and corporate offices to individual pieces designed specifically for client's homes.

Direct contact with clients and collaboration with architects, designers and other artists are welcome.

Existing designs can be adapted in terms of size, materials and function, or entirely new designs may be commissioned.

Coffee Table: 26" x 50" x 17" Pearwood, Holly, Glass; Paintings: Artist Oils.

Peter Handler

Peter Handler Studio
2400 W. Westmoreland Street
Philadelphia, PA 19129
(215) 225-5555 FAX (215) 225-3964

Peter Handler designs and produces custom and limited production anodized aluminum, glass and granite furniture for the home and office. Using high-strength clear adhesives to join metal and glass or stone, he creates furniture which is eminently functional, yet esthetically and structurally minimal.

Working with an excellent commercial anodizer, Handler produces a broad range of colors, frequently developing new hues to meet his clients' needs. Anodized aluminum, with its luminous color spectrum, has a hard, permanent surface that is highly resistant to scratches and stains, retaining its beauty with a minimum of care.

Retail prices range from $1300 for an occasional table to $6000 for a conference table.

Delivery time ranges from two to four months. Catalog and aluminum samples are available upon request.

"Dinner Trolley", 24" x 33" x 29".

"Elemental", Coffee Table, 40" x 48" x 15".

"Chess Master", Chess Table and Chess Set, 30" x 30" x 28".

"Gyro", Coffee Table, 44" x 48" x 14."

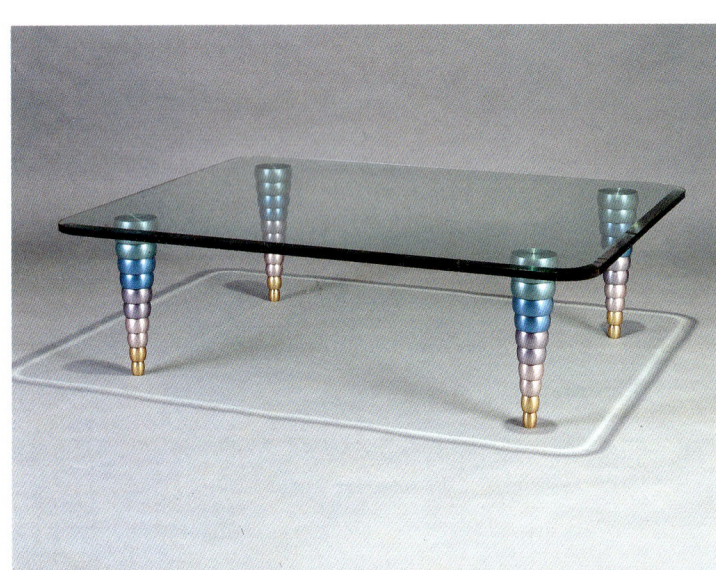

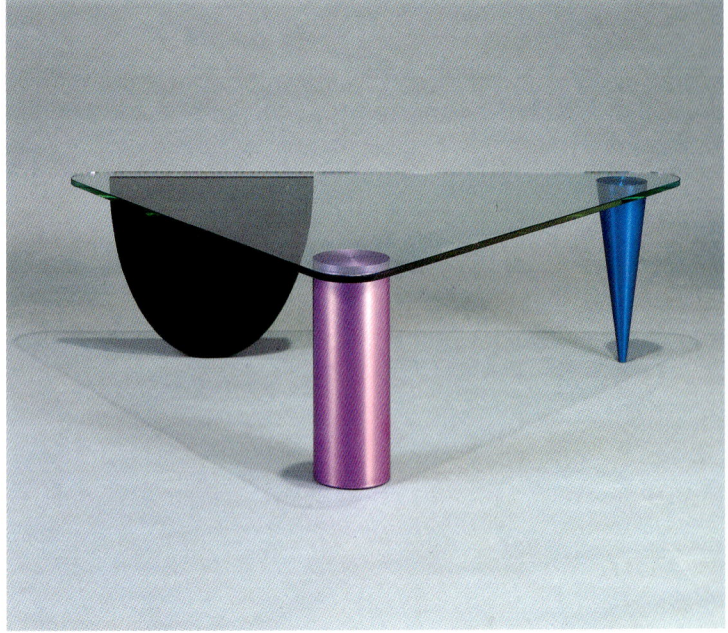

Peter Handler

Peter Handler Studio
2400 W. Westmoreland Street
Philadelphia, PA 19129
(215) 225-5555
(215) 225-3964 FAX

  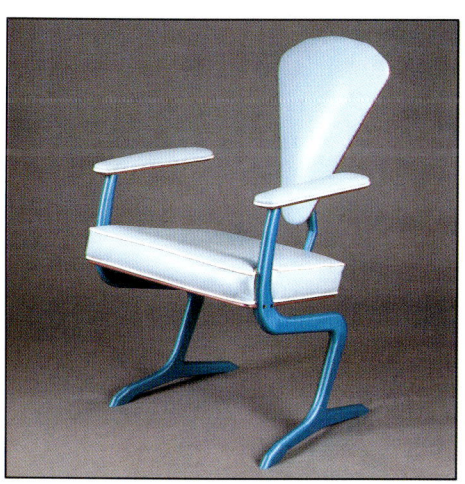

Russell C. Jaqua

Nimba Forge
1119 Blaine St.
Port Townsend, WA 98368
(206) 385-5272

The "Plate Graffique" technique developed by Russell Jaqua is illustrated in the elegant transformation of a durable material, steel, into visually light-active tables.

Over the past seventeen years, Jaqua has exhibited nationally and internationally. He is represented in several museum collections.

The table tops are forged of 1/2" plate, hot worked into a decorative relief; all edges are softened by chamfering. The legs are 1 1/4" forged tapers tenoned through the top.

Harmony among these elements is assured by the process of being wrought.

The Forest and Floral collections portray natural patterns and are offered on a limited production basis. Size and height changes will be accepted on commission. End tables shown with a wax finish are priced at $450 F.O.B.

Noble Fir 16" x 48" x 16" ht.

Wild Rose 16" x 16" x 18" ht.

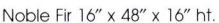

Cherry Blossom 16" x 16" x 18" ht.

104

Rob Johnson

Rob Johnson Furniture
949 Amsterdam Avenue
New York, NY 10025
(212) 865-6027

A self-taught artist with no formal design training, Rob Johnson both designs and executes his line of contemporary furniture. Mr. Johnson's seating, tables and lighting are available in galleries and stores in New York City. Matte Black and Grinded Steel, plate glass and industrial rubber materials ensure strength and durability. Rob Johnson collaborates with glass artist Jerry Morrell and leather artist Toshiki to expand his own skills and to showcase the work of others in his frameworks of steel. Commissions are done promptly and correctly. Retail prices available on request.

(Right) Warrior Lamps—Telescope to 11 ft. tall.

(Below) Adult seating at Soho Gallery location.

John Lewis

John Lewis Glass Studio
1681 Eighth Street
Oakland, CA 94607
(415) 893-3224

The John Lewis Glass Studio creates cast glass sculptures and functional pieces, such as tables and benches which are rendered in a variety of shapes, forms, textures and colors. They also facilitate site-specific architectural projects involving cast, blown, or slumped glass.

During its 20 years in business, the studio has completed a number of commissions for private and corporate clients, and is represented internationally by galleries and art consultants.

Commissioned works can be delivered in three to six months depending on the scale of the project. Sculptural pieces range from $2,500–$7,500; tables and benches range from $7,500–$15,000.

Further information available upon request.

(Top) "Zigzag Table," 33"h x 36"l x 28"w.

(Lower Left) "Gold V-Block Vessel," 15"h x 10"l x 10"w.

(Lower Center) "Compotier," 8"h x 18"l x 18"w.

(Lower Right) "Tangent Vessel," 18"h x 18"l x 7"w.

Ray Lewis

Fauna Collection
P.O. Box 1095
Mariposa, CA 95338
(209) 966-5484

Ray Lewis creates chairs of fantasy and function. They are equally impressive in a corporate collection or residential setting.

The chairs are made of sand-cast aluminum alloy, hand-polished to a fine silver tone. Seats are black leather. Each limited edition chair is numbered and signed by the artist.

They are at once collectible art and fine handcrafted furniture.

The Eagle Chair was the recipient of the 1990 Niche Award for Metal Sculpture. The trio was featured at the Atlantic International Museum of Art and Design.

The Fauna Chairs are shown in numerous galleries and in corporate and private collections throughout the U.S.

Each chair is $2,800. Please allow 4 to 6 weeks for delivery. A brochure is available on request.

(Top) Impala Chair.

(Bottom) Dolphin, Impala and Eagle Designs.

Photography by Marvin Silver.

David MacDonald

12686 C.R. 76
Findlay, OH 45840
(419) 422-1400, 3131

David MacDonald, blacksmith, produces functional and ornamental ironwork for residential and corporate environments, using modern hand forged techniques to achieve traditional results.

MacDonald works closely with architects and potential clients for new design development, and for restoration of architectural ironwork. Specially developed coatings give a wide spectrum of durable finishes.

Installation is available nationwide. A 3 month design and production period is required for major commissions.

A representative portfolio is available upon serious inquiry.

(Top right) Hand forged chess set. Graphite and bronze finishes.

Bruce MacPhail

Highland Woodworks
P.O. Box 22
South Strafford, VT 05070
(802) 785-4364

Bruce MacPhail has been designing and hand building home and office furniture for 15 years. A specialty is diningroom tables; extension tables feature in-table leaf storage. He uses a clean, timeless line and finely finished New England hardwoods. Each piece is signed and numbered.

MacPhail is a member of the League of New Hampshire Craftsmen, the Society of Arts and Crafts, Boston, and the Vermont State Craft Center.

Examples of his work may be seen in *The Guild 1, 2, 4* and *5.*

Brochure available upon request.

(Below) A formal dining table (42"w x 80"l) made of Dakota mahogany, granite, onyx and silver. The base is constructed of oiled cherry with maple detailing. The table was awarded "Best in Show" at the League of New Hampshire Craftsmen Annual Show.

CW Design, Inc.

Carole Wilson Markus
1618 Central Avenue North East
Minneapolis, MN 55413
MN (612) 789-5685
USA 1(800) 328-4827 ext. 1024
FAX (612) 789-0124

Begun in 1974, CW Design's philosophy has always been directed toward promoting the best kind of environment built upon excellence, aesthetics, and sophistication. This is accomplished by blending craftsmanship with design, specializing in architectural glass images appropriate for contemporary as well as more classic traditional spaces.

By integrating mediums such as glass, light and marble as shown in the "shark" table below, CW Design captures the beautiful essence of water.

Photographs available upon request.

Albert Paley

Paley Studios, Ltd.
25 North Washington Street
Rochester, NY 14614
(716) 232-5260 Fax (716) 232-5507

Known for producing large-scale sculpture and a wide range of architecturally related work, Albert Paley and his studio also create individual and unique functional objects in steel and bronze including tables, plant stands, lecterns, door pulls, sconces, and candle holders along with other works of decorative art. All work is designed and produced by Paley Studios.

(Below) © Paley Studios, Ltd. 1990. Series and edition items. Photo by Bruce Miller.

Norman Petersen

350 Treat Avenue
San Francisco, CA 94110
(415) 431-1100

Norman Petersen accepts commissions to design and build pieces for private, commercial, and public spaces. His work includes both interior and outdoor pieces. At present he is working on a series of chairs and tables based on an African tribal motif. His work is shown in galleries throughout the U.S. and is in the permanent collection of the San Francisco Museum of Modern Art. Contact Norman Petersen's Studio for information on pricing and current exhibitions.

born–1941

Stanford University, Academy of Art in Munich, San Francisco Art Institute.

1966–79 Designer, Teacher, Builder in California and France.

1979–present Designs and builds furniture in his San Francisco studio.

Norman Petersen
350 Treat Avenue
San Francisco, CA 94110
(415) 431-1100

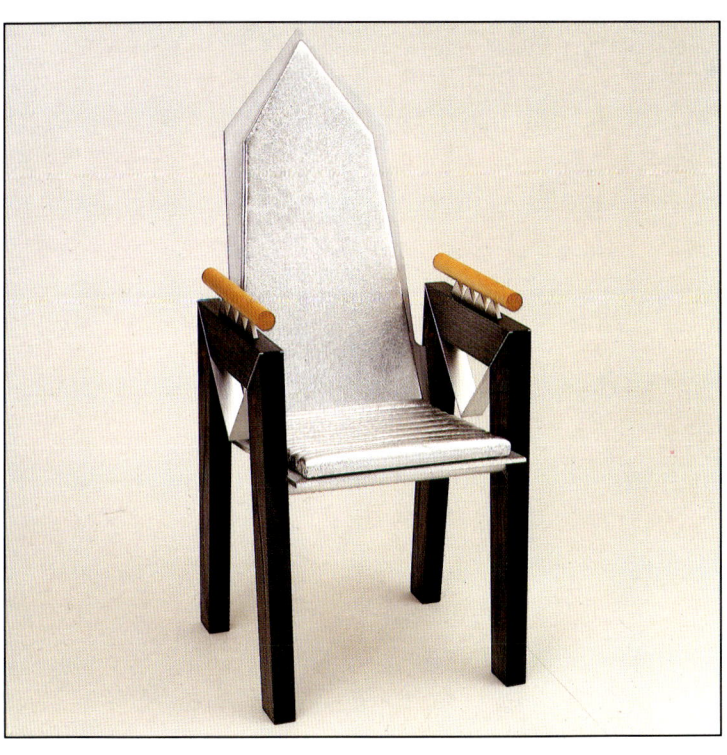

David A. Ponsler

Wonderland Products, Inc.
5772 Lenox Avenue
P.O. Box 6074
Jacksonville, FL 32236
(904) 786-0144
FAX (904) 786-0145

David Ponsler's hand forged "bed of roses" features heavy twisted bars and delicate ribbons and roses. It is finished in natural oils and waxes which allow the inherent beauty of the iron to show through.

This model is queen size and retails for $16,000.00. Please inquire for information and pricing on other sizes, variations and custom designs.

David Ponsler also does a wide variety of architectural metal products for which you can request literature.

Southwest inquiries should be directed to Hargett Associates/Dallas, Houston.

Brian F. Russell

Brian Russell Designs
2537 Broad Avenue
Memphis, TN 38112
(901) 327-1210

Brian Russell excels in creating exciting and original forged steel furniture and architectural details for interior designers, architects, corporations and private clients. Based on historical precedents and constructed with a dedication to craft and materials, the limited edition tables are priced from $1500–4000. Gates, railings and screens may be finished for interior or exterior use and are priced on an individual basis. Installation is available throughout the U.S. Other products include door handles, knockers, fireplace accessories, sculpture, candelabrums, lighting and other architectural and furniture pieces. Brian Russell's work is shown on both coasts, with a listing and portfolio available.

(Shown here) Monologue Table, steel and marble, 20" x 24" x 27", Phyllis Morris, Beverly Hills

Carolyn Sale

Carolyn Sale Ceramic Sculpture
2044 Hoover Avenue
Oakland, CA 94602
(415) 530-2228

Ceramic table bases designed and hand crafted by California artist Carolyn Sale are the ultimate in artistic furniture.

These unique tables strike a perfect balance of contemporary design and function. They capture a full range of colors that are softly blended with each other through a variety of air-brushing techniques. An exterior transparent glaze adds durability.

Delightfully elegant, these sculptural tables are a dramatic addition to any home or office.

Production time is approximately 12 weeks. Prices begin at $2,000.

Jeffrey Sass

Jeffrey Sass: Metal Work
231 Quechee-W. Hartford Road
White River Jct., VT 05001
(802) 295-6689

The Nursery Rhyme Mirror is a harmony of one client's cherished rhymes and memorabilia and Sass's interplay of machined steel gunparts.

Innovative solutions in metal. Inquiries welcomed.

Mirrors from $750. Beds from $3,000. Brochure on request.

Jeffrey Sass integrates industrial scrapmetal, antique castings and sentimental bric-a-brac into heirloom-quality art furnishings.

This queensize bed of matte black steel incorporates two antique summercovers from Savannah. Each one-of-a-kind creation reflects something of the client or setting, be it gracious southern style, city chic or stately Adirondack repose.

117

Martha Sears

P.O. Box 1153
Washington Green, CT 06793
(413) 567-7433

Martha Sears designs and builds provocative table sculptures using mixed media—ceramics, glass, wood and plastics. Visually intriguing and challenging one's sense of balance yet structurally sound. Pieces range from game tables to coffee tables to runners to conference tables.

A portfolio is available upon request. Commissions are accepted.

(Right) Commission, chess table, mixed media, 29"x32"x32", Springfield, MA.

(Below left) Coffee table, mixed media, 50"x30"x27".

(Below right) Installation, side table (foreground) and coffee table (background).

Steve Smith

Smithwork Studio
13691 State, Route 249
Ney, OH 43549
(419) 658-2812

Unyielding materials like stone and steel become functional sculpture in the studio of Steve Smith. His enthusiasm and awareness of symbolism are evident in his work. Smith designs tables of steel and stone (from quarry slate to Baroque marble). Custom designs are available, made to a client's order.

Trained as a sculptor, Smith has been working with clay, stone, and steel to produce decorative, functional, and architectural work for more than 16 years.

His current experiments include adding wood to some of his tables and wallpieces.

Prices for stone and steel tables begin at $500.

(Top) Sandwich table, slate, forged and fabricated steel, 25" high, $800.

(Bottom) Dolmen table, slate and forged steel, 26" high, $500.

Jay Stanger

Modern Methods Design
465 Medford Street
Charlestown, MA 02129
(617) 242-5200

For the past 11 years, Jay Stanger has been creating abstract, interactive sculpture which meets the challenge of both functional and fine art.

Combining the strength and versatility of metal with the richness of exotic wood, Stanger's painstaking attention to construction, detail and use of traditional joinery methods ensure a long and durable life for each unique piece. Such exacting standards have earned the artist a reputation for honoring commitments without sacrificing quality.

Recognized for the originality of his design in such publications as the *New York Times* and *Architectural Record*, Stanger's work has been exhibited nationally and is included in the Smithsonian Institute's traveling exhibition of handmade furniture and the Boston Museum of Fine Arts' permanent collection.

(This page) "Times of Day", liquor cabinet, 42"w x 103"h x 22"d.

(Opposite, top left) "Twisting Table", pau amarillo, anodized aluminum, cast epoxy resin, 42" diameter.

(Top right) Bench, purpleheart, maple, aluminum, 45"w x 22"h x 18"d.

(Center right) Hollywood chair, holly, ebony, aluminum, epoxy, fiber, 36"w x 35"h x 25"d.

(Bottom) Bridge set, table 36" diameter; chairs, various woods, anodized aluminum, acrylic, 21"w x 36"h x 18"d.

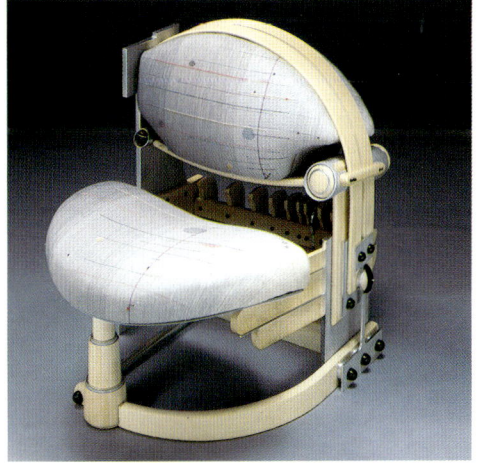

Mamie Spiegel

147 West 15 Street
New York, NY 10011
(212) 675-4972

Shown here are a few of the wide variety of tables Mamie Spiegel makes. Made of clay tiles affixed to a sturdy plywood base, each piece comes with a set of plates handmade to complement the table.

The standard tables measure approximately 3 ft. by 6 ft., and seat six people; but they can be built to any dimensions required.

Her work has appeared in numerous magazines, books and galleries. She received an NEA grant, and her work has been featured in two shows at the American Craft Museum in New York.

Spiegel also collaborates with designers and architects on fireplaces, doorways, bathrooms and other tile installations.

The price of a table seating six and matching plates is $3,600. For further information, please contact the artist.

Brian Swanson

727 16th Avenue West
Kirkland, WA 98033
(206) 827-0398

Represented By
MIA Gallery
314 Occidental Ave. South
Seattle, WA 98104
(206) 467-8283

Brian Swanson's vision is inspired by the cast off machine parts, tools, and appliances that he collects. His designs highlight the function and beauty of parts made during an earlier time, proving durable for indoors or out.

Surprise, innovation, humor, and elegance can be found in his pieces.

A strong sense of design is evident along with a straightforward handling of materials.

Collaboration with design teams are welcome. Timelines negotiable.

Prices range $800-$4,000.

(Top) Writing Chair.   (Bottom) Counsel Chair.

Photos by Eduardo Calderon © 1990.

J. Anthony Ulinski

Dovetail Woodworks, Est. 1976
24 Commerce Place
Raleigh, NC 27601
(919) 832-4529

Anthony Ulinski uses traditional joinery, bent laminations and composites to create one-of-a-kind and limited edition pieces for commercial installations, residences and individual collectors. He works in all woods and finishes including dyes, lacquers and laminates.

Typical works include chairs, side tables and conference room tables up to 24' in length, as well as entire boardroom interiors. Projects are individually designed, with prices and delivery schedule available upon request. Installation and consultation are also available.

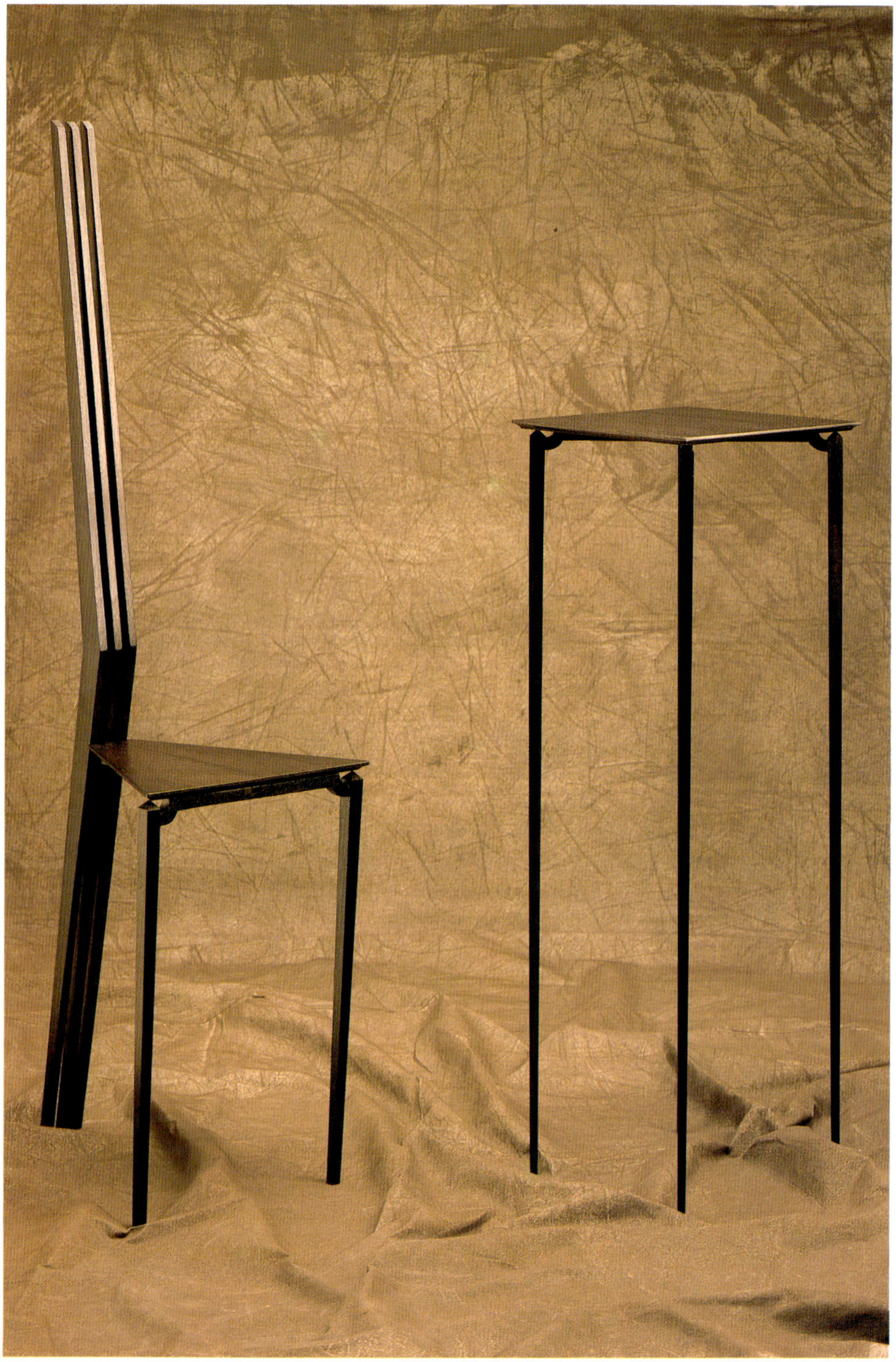

Gary Upton

Gary Upton Woodworking inc.
12856 Loma Rica Drive
Grass Valley, CA 95945
(916) 273-1449

Combining Hardwoods, Granite, and Metals, Gary Upton creates furniture that is on the cutting edge of design and function.

Since 1976 Gary's work has been featured in Fine woodworking, Northern California Home and Garden, and Sacramento KCRA-TV Evening Magazine.

Custom Commission/Limited Production, brochure and price list are available.

Audio System (Bottom) 89" x 24" x 79h" in figured maple, granite, anodized aluminum, ebony & ebonized mahogany. The upper cabinet hinges from back to access connections.

Hall Table (top) 30" x 18" x 36h" granite, maple, ebonized mahogany.

Larry Alan White

Vista Pacific Studios
664 South Coast Highway
Laguna Beach, CA 92651
(619) 940-6384

Larry Alan White's ability to envision and craft contemporary, functional objects of art has earned him the respect and praise of both clients and peers.

A seven-year apprenticeship with preeminent woodworker Sam Maloof influenced White's background in fine arts. His most widely known pieces dramatize an extraordinary balance of mediums—unique combinations of domestic and foreign hardwoods, elegantly coupled with aluminum, copper, glass and other unexpected materials.

With projects ranging from jewelry and furniture to the building of custom homes, White is equally comfortable as sole designer or as a team collaborator.

His work has been exhibited nationally and is included in both private and public collections.

(Top) Tri-Point Series #4, 24"w x 16"h, wenge, ebony, Osage orange, aluminum.

(Bottom) Tri-Point Series #6, 24" x 16"h, wenge, ebony, blood wood, Osage orange, aluminum.

Wooldridge Sculpture Studios

Stephen E. Wooldridge
1264 West 206 Street
Sheridan, IN 46069
(317) 758-6076

Stephen E. Wooldridge has been working in metal for over 30 years. He has studied Design and Sculpture at Dayton Art Institute and advanced Sculpture technique at Herron Art Institute. He has extensive experience in the welding, fabrication and finishing of ferrous, non-ferrous metals, and exotic alloys through training with the US Navy. His work has been viewed through out Northern America and Europe.

He is currently building limited edition sculptural furniture, and site specific sculpture for indoors and out.

Stephen works closely with architects, designers, and private clients and is able to handle all aspects of design, construction, transportation and installation.

Brochures and additional details are available upon request.

PAINTED FURNITURE

3

William Adair

Gold Leaf Studios
443 1 Street, NW
Washington, DC 20001
(202) 638-4660
(202) 347-4569 FAX

Specializing in the conservation of gilded antiques, Gold Leaf Studios has offered a full complement of gilding and frame-related services to museums, collectors and designers for over a decade.

The Studio is equipped to handle frame fabrication, specialty matting and frame reproductions of carved wood and composition. The studio also offers its own contemporary frame styles, plus a selection of period frames from its private collection. Time honored traditional techniques are used by the Studio's craftsmen to conserve delicate patinas on valuable gilded antiques such as furniture and sculpture. Interior and exterior gilding is a specialty and includes cornices, panelled rooms, medallions and other architectural embellishments.

(Top) Detail of a ceiling in the Diplomatic Reception Rooms at the State Department.

(Bottom left) Gilded chair ca. 1820 from public collection.

(Bottom right) Reproduction of antique composition frame.

Laura Bender
John Early

Site Painters
4851 Palm Avenue
La Mesa, CA 91941
(619) 462-0159

John Early and Laura Bender create fine
art images in a folding screen format for
residential and commercial settings in
collaboration with designers, architects, and
private clients. Bender and Early work in
a range of styles from painterly to collage-
inspired, using representational, abstract, and
folk-art motifs.

Their wood screens are of fine furniture quality
and sealed for durability. Screen proportions,
number of panels, etc. are part of the artist/
client design process. Prices start at $1500.
and include a 3-D scale model.

Site Painters also produces murals, panels,
stencils, and paint finishes. Complete
information is available.

All screens shown, 6 1/2'h x 5'w, wood and
acrylic paint.

Lib & Eric Cummings

Represented by: Joan Robey Gallery
939 Broadway
Denver, CO 80203
(303) 892-9600

Lib and Eric Cummings are graduates of the Rhode Island School of Design. Inspired by their diverse interests in art history, ancient cultures, mysticism and fantasy, they create commissioned furnishings and environments including columns, pedestals, tables, seating, screens and panels.

Eric, a registered architect, provides working drawings and technical specifications. Lib, an accomplished painter and illustrator, collaborates on design elements and motifs.

The painted images are applied either to the direct surface or a "frescoed" finish.

Design and fabrication time varies from 4–12 weeks.

A brochure with price list is available upon request.

(Top left) Southwest environment.

(Top right) "Dancing" chairs with needlepoint seats.

(Bottom) "Desert" dining table and "Howling Coyote" coffee table.

Laura Dabrowski

LAURA D'S
Folk Art Furniture, Inc.
106 Gleneida Avenue
Carmel, NY 10512
(914) 228-1440

"Playfulness and creativity join with superior craftmanship in the world of Laura Dabrowski." Indianapolis Museum of Art

Laura Dabrowski, a.k.a. "Laura D", goes for more pizzazz." Maggie Malone, *Newsweek*

Laura D. brings humor and an unmistakable presence to the world of handpainted childrens furniture. Her durable line of birchwood cows and cats, rabbits and bull terriers as well as bowlegged roosters and more was inaugurated with the birth of her son Cody. Each piece features bold brush work and fabric like patterns.

Laura D's work can be seen at FAO Schwarz, Neiman Marcus, and many fine stores and galleries. Prices from $100.00 to $10,000 for an outdoor play house. A color brochure is available for $2.00. Adult size pieces are also available.

2nd Place Furniture Award, Bruce Museum, Greenich, CT.

133

Clark Ellefson

Lewis & Clark
1231 Lincoln Street
Columbia, SC 29201
(803) 765-2405

Lewis & Clark's witty and meticulously crafted sculptural furniture has won many awards, including the Formica International Design Competition. Their fresh, often whimsical, vision has earned them showings in the Salon De Mobile, the Victoria and Albert Museum, the Miami Museum of Modern Art, and the Chicago Art Institute (permanent collection). Their designs have appeared in many publications, including *Casa Vogue*, *Pronto* (Japanese design magazine), *Architecture*, *Interiors*, and *Architectural Record*.

Typical is the Kimono Cabinet pictured (57"w x 58"h x 12"d), now part of the permanent collection of the South Carolina Arts Commission. The cabinet is finished on all sides. Each one in the series is a different pattern with a base price of $4,000. (Subject to change.)

Other sculptural objects for sale include modestly priced lamps and accessories. Dealers welcome.

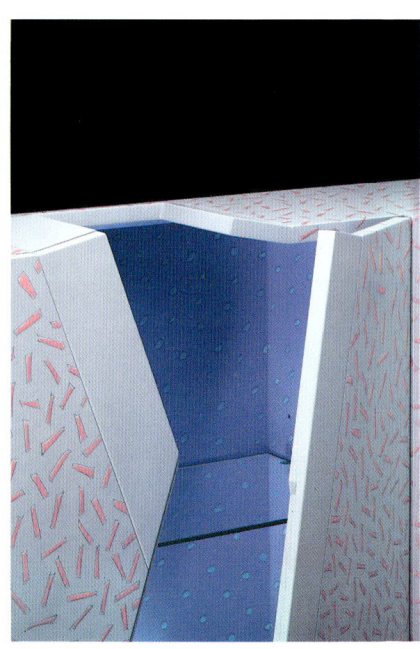

Joel W. Evett
Roberta L. Boylen

Evett & Boylen Furniture
226 Beech Street
Belmont, MA 02178
(617) 484-2539

Evett and Boylen create classic contemporary furniture. Their style unites cabinetry of fine design and construction with narrative imagery, panel paintings, relief sculpture and shadowboxes. While employing the finest traditional and modern techniques, great attention is given to all aspects of their work. From the designing of a cornice molding, the turning of a foot, the gilding of a detail to the final egg tempera glaze of an image, quality and longevity is the artists' goal.

The artists create one-of-a-kind pieces and limited editions. Commissions are accepted.

(Left) Pompeii Cabinet: 5'3" x 34" x 22", aphromosia, wenge, maple, egg tempera.

(Right bottom) Pompeii Cabinet: interior.

(Right top) Mackerel Cabinet: 7'2" x 28" x 22", maple, birdseye maple, egg tempera, gold leaf.

Johanna Okovic Goodman

Okovic / Goodman Studio
718 S. 22nd Street
Philadelphia, PA 19146
(215) 546-1448

Johanna Okovic-Goodman uses "found chairs" to create functional sculpture. These wood chairs are built up directly with acrylic medium or stuffed and painted to create a unique objet.

The colors are protected with multiple coats of polyurethane. Goodman's color and execution are of the highest quality. Only natural wood chairs are used. The Santa Fe and Folk Art styles featured employ mixed media: ribbon, fabric, beads, hemp, oil cloth, and hand-made paper. All add to the three-dimensional qualities without sacrificing functionality.

Clients can use their own chairs or the artist will supply them. Prices range from $250 to $800. Two week delivery.

Goodman's work is featured in galleries and stores across the country.

Photos by Robert Goodman.

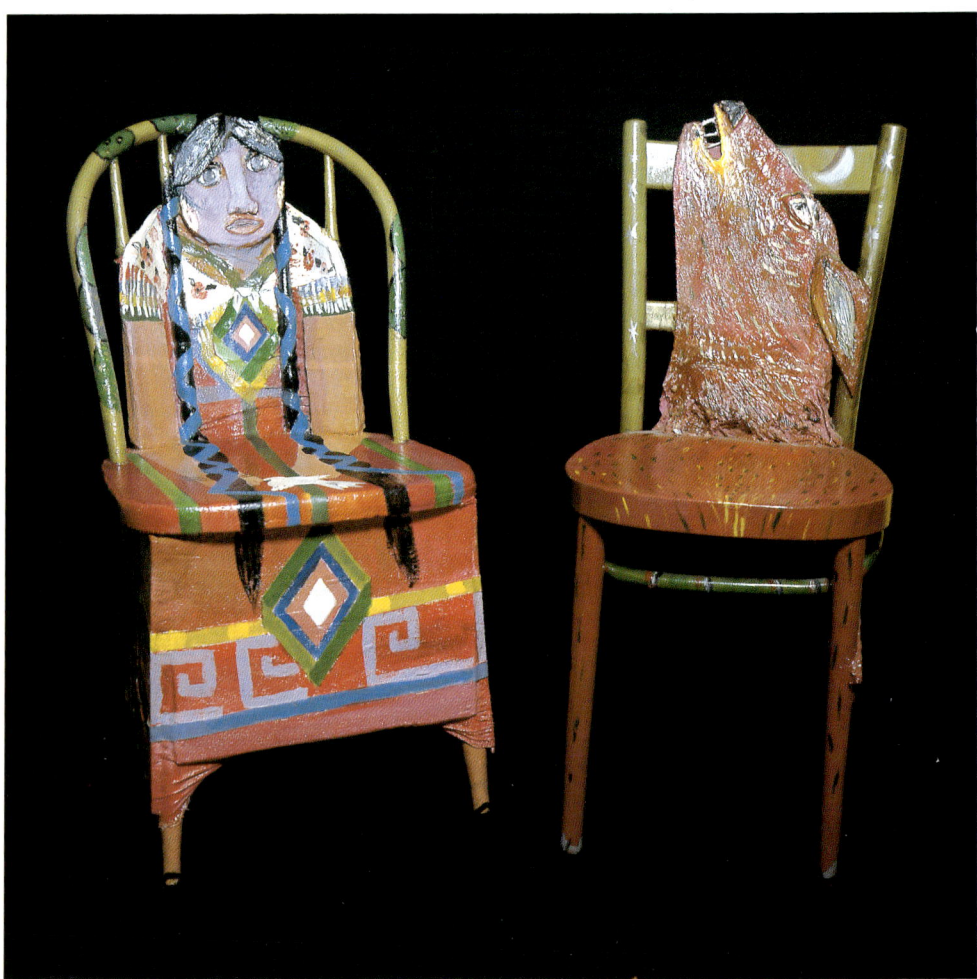

Johanna Okovic Goodman

Okovic/Goodman Studio
718-B South 22nd Street
Philadelphia, PA 19146-1105
(215) 546-1448

(Upper right) Jaguar (l), Coyote (r) Front View.

(Lower right) Coyote (l), Jaguar (r) Rear View.

Yoshi Hayashi

351 Ninth Street, 3rd Floor
San Francisco, CA 94103
(415) 552-0755, (415) 924-9224

Yoshi Hayashi creates twentieth century interpretations of traditional Japanese lacquer art, with a keen awareness of the finest details. He produces a wide variety of original designs, which range from traditional to modern. His designs on screens, boxes, furniture and decorative objects are contemporary reflections of Hayashi's Japanese heritage.

His work has been exhibited in the V. Brier Gallery, Gump's and Neiman-Marcus in San Francisco, Nikko Hotel and Galleria Design Center's shears & window.

Commissions are accepted.

138

Peter Malakoff
Norman Jones

Malakoff & Jones
Schoonmaker Building
10 Liberty Ship Way #4139
Sausalito, CA 94965
(415) 332-7471
(415) 332-2481 FAX

Peter Malakoff and Norman Jones have designed and built art cabinetry and furniture in the San Francisco area for the past eight years. With their knowledge and appreciation of both ancient and foreign cultures, they demonstrate in their work a distinctive interplay between craft and fine art, with a sensitive attention to detail.

They welcome innovative commissions from the architectural, corporate and private worlds.

Pictures of "Egypto-Deco Pharaoh Cabinet," inspired by objects found in Tutankhamun's tomb. Privately commissioned. Completed 1/8/89. 120"w (180"w open) x 90"h x 28"d. Materials: Sycamore, satinwood, ebony, ivory, gold, lacquer.

Gregory Sheres

Gregory Sheres Studio
9902 NW 52nd Terrace
Miami, FL 33178
(305) 477-4200

Greg Sheres brings fine art to furniture, For a canvas, the artist uses such materials as emerald pearl granite imported from Sweden and travertine marble imported from Italy. Every table is cut by the artist's own hand; an original painting is then applied to the stone, and then finished with lasting layers of acrylic resin. Heavy stainless steel is then shaped, molded and welded to form a one of a kind base as inspired by the table top.

The artist works closely with clients to incorporate their custom specifications.

Allow 2–3 months for completion of project.

Brochure available upon request.

Prices range from $1,900–$11,000.

Travertine console table, 60" x 18" x 29".

White marble end table, 32" x 22" x 19".

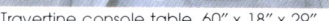

Granite cocktail table, 68" x 38" x 17".

Christian Thee

49 Old Stagecoach Road
Weston, CT 06883
(203) 454-0340

Trained as a theatrical designer and master scenic artist, Christian Thee has been acknowledged as one of the top trompe l'oeil technicians of his time. His deliberate theatrical style has been incorporated into private and corporate commissions which include restaurant and hotel murals and architectural trompe l'oeil.

His work is both mysterious and romantic. It draws the viewer in and invites them to find the intricate surprises that highlight his painterly inventions.

Examples of his artistry have been featured in the store windows of Tiffany & Company, while larger works include the ceilings for Buccellatti in Trump Tower, New York City, murals in the dining room of the Merridien Hotel in New Orleans and a forty-six foot Persian mural for Trump's Taj Majal in Atlantic City.

Shown here are two trompe l'oeil table tops measuring approximately 18" across. Also available are obelisk–shaped cat houses, console tables embelished with trompe l'oeil articles, and decorative screens.

Since much of Mr. Thee's work is custom, inquiries are always welcome.

ARCHITECTURAL WOODWORK

4

Ian Agrell
Adam Thorpe

Agrell and Thorpe
British Classical Carvers
1301 Wazee Street
Denver, CO 80204
(303) 825-6416

British Master Carver, Mr. Ian Agrell and Chief Carver, Adam Thorpe together with their staff create traditional hand carved decoration for architecture and furniture to the highest European standards.

The workshop has undertaken commissions for such major British establishments as Kensington Palace, Ely Cathedral, the new Lloyd's Building in the City of London, and Trinity College of Music.

Their work also graces the residences and palaces of the Sultan of Brunei, the Sultan of Oman, the King of Jordan and includes commissions for the Saudi Royal family.

For an estimate of cost, send photographs or drawings of your project. Mr. Agrell will collaborate on design and install work anywhere in the world.

Stephen M. Cabitt

Stephen M. Cabitt Company
Cabinetmakers/Designers
97 Strathmore Road
Brookline, MA 02146
(617) 734-4286

Stephen Cabitt has designed and built furniture for architects and designers in the Boston/New York area for the past fifteen years. He is comfortable working in a classic or contemporary format and enjoys collaborating with other designers. His commercial installation experience is invaluable on large scale pieces.

Projects range from breakfronts and armoires to limited production of contract furniture for corporate clients. Libraries are a specialty.

Historical commissions include the Old Corner Bookstore for the Boston Globe, the Paul Revere House, Isabella Stuart Gardner Museum, and Museum of Transportation.

He is pleased to review drawings and provide prompt quotations. A brochure is available upon request.

(Upper right), Old Corner Bookstore, Boston, MA.

Mahogany Corner Cupboard.

Randy Cochran

Wood Studio
Route 3 Box 427
Decatur, AL 35603
(205) 350-5270

A woodworker for 15 years, Randy Cochran builds custom cabinets and furniture from his own original designs and collaborative designs.

Working in solid hardwood, fine veneers, plastic laminates, metals, leather, glass, marble and synthetic stone, Cochran produces desks, tables, chairs, case goods, office furniture and cabinets.

The collaborative designs pictured are made of mahogany with surfaces of green marble and burgundy leather, custom matched to the client's office space. Credenza, 3½' x 7' oval; desk, 2½' x 10'. Cabinet in background, mahogany and glass.

A brochure, photos, slides and references are available upon request. Collaborative work is welcome.

Thomas J. Duffy

Duffy's General & Specific Millwork
52 E. River Street
Ogdensburg, NY 13669
(315) 393-8553
Fax (315) 393-4827

Studio crafts are alive, well and available from Tom Duffy. From one-of-a-kind designs and fabrications to collaborations with other crafts artist, promise is made good.

Duffy's range of work is from design/build furniture (see furniture page) to unusual architectural woodworking and boat building.

More information upon request.

(Clockwise) Set of radius doors with curved glass side lites.
Walnut and poplar, 7'h x 9'w, 1988.

Cabinetry that floats: A St. Lawrence River/Rowing Skiff. Fiberglass hull, wood seats, decks and bed, brass trim, Length· 18'3", 1989.

Al Garvey

DOOR/WAYS
281 Scenic Road
Fairfax, CA 94930
(415) 453-5275

Each door created in Al Garvey's studio is expressly designed to reflect the architectural and interior elements of a specific home or business. A unique combination of design, materials, color and finish contributes to the elegance of every door.

The many possibilities include contemporary textured or faux finishes, exotic hardwoods finished to enhance their natural beauty, all forms of stained, etched and leaded glass and metal work including custom-designed knobs and levers.

All doors are frame and panel construction with mortise and tenon joints throughout. Garvey enjoys collaborating with clients, architects and designers, especially since the inspiration for each door is the lifestyle expressed in the architecture and interior design.

Photographs and brochures are available upon request.

(All photos) Three of Garvey's recent creations in situs.

148

Boyd A. Hutchison

Hutchison Woodworking
P.O. Box 928 (Route 7)
Sheffield, MA 01257
(413) 229-3280

Boyd Hutchison builds custom furniture one piece at a time utilizing timeless Shaker designs which are faithfully reproduced or thoughtfully adapted for contemporary living. The finest domestic cabinet woods are used in his furniture along with traditional, time-tested joinery of uncompromised quality and flawless, hand-rubbed finishes which produce durable surfaces that enhance the beauty of the fine woods used.

Installation services are available for built-in pieces. Send for brochure.

(Top right) Canterbury side table reproduction.

(Bottom) The Shaker Wall at Round Hill Farm.

149

Dimitrios Klitsas

705 Union Street
West Springfield, MA 01089
(413) 732-2661

For every designer, architect and interior decorator dedicated to exclusive homes and memorable interior appointments, exists Dimitrios Klitsas to fulfill and to surpass their every wood carving vision.

You are cordially invited to discover custom-designed, meticulously hand-carved furnishings of elegance.

Tables, chairs, beds, mirrors, entrances and walls are lovingly crafted for discriminating tastes and opulent surroundings.

Lavish works are created for private, corporate and ecclesiastical circles.

Dimitrios Klitsas

705 Union Street
West Springfield, MA 01089
(413) 732-2661

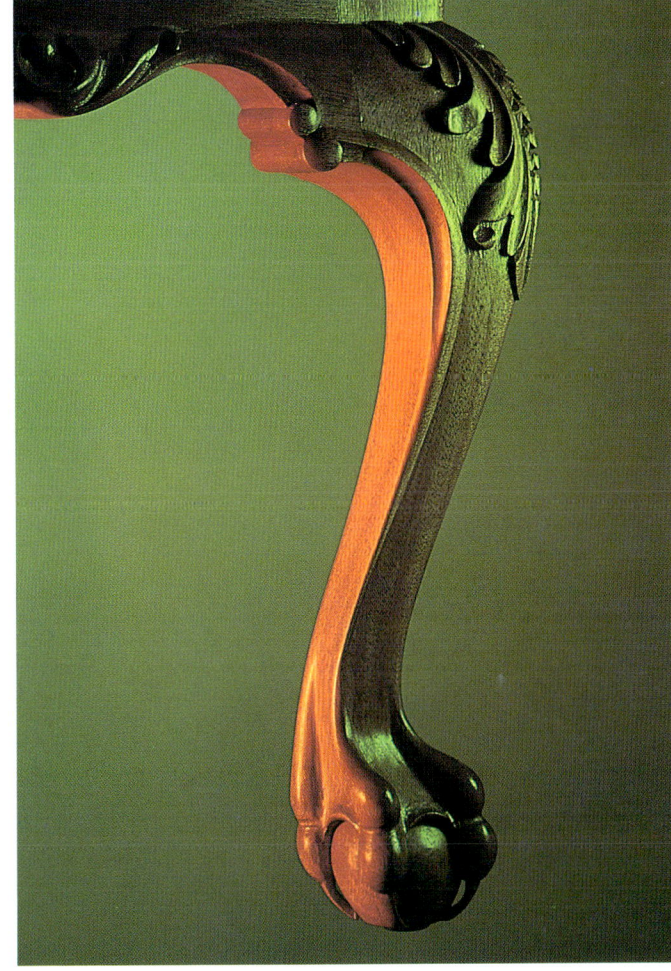

Jerry Lilly

R.J. Casey Ind. Park
Columbus and Preble
Pittsburgh, PA 15233
(412) 322-8950

Jerry Lilly's handmade furniture and cabinetry, often featuring designs hand carved from the mass, are suited for corporate and residential environments. The original designs are executed from fine materials with keen attention to detail.

Lilly holds a master's degree from Indiana University of Pennsylvania.

(Top left) "Amen! Aten!", Honduras mahogany and walnut, 18" w x 32" h x 9"d.

(Top right) "Prelude", Honduras mahogany and walnut, 18"w x 32"h x 9"d.

(Bottom) New York City kitchen in cherry.

Rodger Reid

Wood Interiors by Rodger Reid
Marbledale, CT 06777
(203) 868-7706

Rodger Reid creates timeless elegance with his panelled rooms and libraries for residential and commercial interiors.

Committed to the highest quality standards, Reid hand selects only the world's finest hardwood to complement his designs. All work is done by hand in the tradition of master craftsmen of past centuries.

A natural oil finish is hand rubbed and then waxed to bring out the beauty of the wood, which gathers warmth over the years.

For more than 20 years, Reid has been collaborating with architects, designers, antique dealers and homeowners in the United States and Canada. His work has appeared in *Architectural Digest, House Beautiful, Colonial Homes, House and Garden* and *Country Living*.

Robert Sterba

Robert Sterba Studio
12000 Prospect NE
Albuquerque, NM 87112
(505) 265-6197

Viewing columns and their components as the ultimate interior element, Robert Sterba delights in adding the crowning touch to an environment.

From classical to fanciful, columns may stand on their own or as sculpture and plant stands.

Soft sandblasted pines glazed in desert colors, unusual sponged lacquers, stone finishes, fractured ruins or straight from space...

Please write for more information;
Robert Sterba Studio
COLUMNS • PEDESTALS • FURNITURE.

The Century Guild

Nick Strange
PO Box 13128
Research Triangle Park NC 27709
(919) 598-1612

By commission: design, fabrication, installation of exceptional one-of-a-kind contemporary or traditional pieces for corporate, residential or ecclesiastical spaces. Brochure upon request.

(Top right) Curved Section: architect-designed boardtable for Glaxo Inc. (27' by 12'; mahogany, cherry, marble).

(Bottom right) Upper Portion: architect-designed columbarium cabinet for Saint Thomas Church Fifth Avenue (New York, NY), showing triple-door detail (quarter-sawn white oak, mahogany, ebony).

(Below) Corner Detail: executive desk (ash, olive ash burl, ebony).

CRAFT ARTISTS AND COMPANIES INDEX

PHOTO CREDITS